By Therese Harasymiw

SLAVERY
IN THE
NEW WORLD

Cavendish Square

New York

Published in 2022 by Cavendish Square Publishing, LLC, 29 E. 21st Street
New York, NY 10010

Copyright © 2022 by Cavendish Square Publishing, LLC

First Edition

Portions of this work were originally authored by Don Nardo and published as *The Atlantic
Slave Trade* (*Lucent Library of Black History*). All new material this edition authored by
Therese Harasymiw.

All websites were available and accurate when this book was sent to press.

Library of Congress Cataloging-in-Publication Data

Names: Harasymiw, Therese, author.
Title: Slavery in the New World / Therese Harasymiw.
Description: New York : Cavendish Square Publishing, [2022] | Series:
Turning points | Includes bibliographical references and index.
Identifiers: LCCN 2020034822 | ISBN 9781502660879 (library binding) | ISBN
9781502660862 (paperback) | ISBN 9781502660886 (ebook)
Subjects: LCSH: Slavery—America—History—Juvenile literature. | Slave
trade—America—History—Juvenile literature. |
Slaves—America—History—Juvenile literature.
Classification: LCC HT1048 .H428 2022 | DDC 306.3/62097—dc23
LC record available at https://lccn.loc.gov/2020034822

Editor: Therese Shea
Copy Editor: Abby Young
Designer: Deanna Paternostro

Some of the images in this book illustrate individuals who are models. The depictions do not
imply actual situations or events.

CPSIA compliance information: Batch #CS22CSQ: For further information contact Cavendish Square Publishing LLC, New York,
New York, at 1-877-980-4450.

Printed in the United States of America

Find us on

TABLE OF CONTENTS

INTRODUCTION

A TERRIBLE PART OF HISTORY

In 2007, the United Nations established March 25 as the International Day of Remembrance of the Victims of Slavery and the Transatlantic Slave Trade. The organization believed it was important to set aside time for people to remember, honor, and mourn the millions who endured slavery and the slave trade so many years ago. Lasting for more than 300 years, the transatlantic slave trade reduced human beings to goods, all in the name of so-called economic progress in the "New World," better known today as the Americas. Although the slave trade ended in the 19th century, its effects are still felt today. Only by learning about it and about the lives of enslaved people can we better comprehend this tragic part of history—and discover how it still affects us today.

The transatlantic slave trade, called this because it crossed the Atlantic Ocean, arose in the late 1400s and was not dismantled until the early 1800s. Even then, smuggling enslaved Africans into the United States is known to have occurred into the 1860s. This slave trade, which involved transporting captured Africans to both North and South America, was just one segment of the broader economic scheme called the triangular trade. Historical evidence has revealed that goods such as weapons, cloth products, and alcohol from Europe were shipped to Africa, where the items were traded for African people. Then, these enslaved Africans were taken on ships to the Americas, where they worked on plantations, on smaller farms, in

◀ From the moment of their capture in Africa, enslaved people endured a life of difficulty and heartbreak.

households, and in many businesses and trades without pay and with few basic human rights. The products produced by slave labor, such as sugar and tobacco, were then taken back to European ports. This completed the triangle of trade set up among Europe, Africa, and the Americas, a practice that left a trail of human suffering in its wake.

Investigating the Numbers

Studying the transatlantic slave trade is difficult because of incomplete and sometimes inaccurate records. In recent years, historians have made remarkable strides in collecting and vetting information for a more precise understanding of the numbers. For example, three years of work by librarians, scholars, cartographers, computer programmers, web designers, and other professionals in Europe, Africa, North America, and South America created a comprehensive database containing information about the transatlantic slave trade. Information about more than 36,000 voyages is accessible on the Trans-Atlantic Slave Trade Database (slavevoyages.org), revealing that about 12,520,000 enslaved Africans were taken from their continent and about 10,700,000 survived and disembarked, mostly in the Americas. The data also reveals that hundreds of ships sank or had some other misfortune before reaching Africa, and hundreds befell the same fate after leaving Africa with kidnapped Africans onboard. The database acknowledges that other sources believe the number of enslaved Africans taken to the New World is higher, perhaps more than 15 million people. If this is true, that means many records have been lost, are inexact, or have been falsified over the years. Even with the lower estimated numbers, the facts show that at least three times more enslaved Africans than Europeans arrived in the New World before 1820. This startling statistic compels students of history to realize that the history of the Americas is tightly entwined with the history of the transatlantic slave trade.

Even the most accurate data about the numbers of enslaved people and slave ships—as shocking as they might be—could never reflect the human experience of an enslaved person. It is impossible to fully understand the depth of suffering, hopelessness, and abuse that these Africans experienced by simply looking at numbers. There is no doubt that the legacy of the transatlantic slave trade will forever haunt humanity. It was one of the most destructive events in history, and the descendants of the Africans who were ripped from their homes still feel the effects of the evil institution. The lives of their ancestors were sacrificed so that the empires of Europe could spread.

Perspectives

In general, Americans and Europeans learn about slavery and the slave trade in school—and agree that these practices were morally wrong and unjustified. However, the idea that many successful modern nations, including the United States, were built partly on the labors of enslaved millions is still not widely acknowledged by white people. Often, the manner in which white Americans and Europeans view the slave trade differs from the way the descendants of the enslaved Africans see it. According to an article on the African history and culture website called African Holocaust:

> To many white people, slavery and colonialism are just a distant memory of a short period in history. In Britain and the United States, many whites believe that slavery did not last particularly long, its benefits went only to a small proportion of white people and the evils of slavery are overshadowed by the role played by British abolitionists.

> To people of African descent though, the memory is a very different one. Slavery and colonialism affect everyday lives and evoke poignant and immediate memories of suffering, brutalisation and terror. The memories are of Britain and the USA achieving their economic prosperity on the back of African enslavement ... Many people believe that the racism that grew out of African enslavement is the reason for today's racial inequalities.[1]

Many white people assume that the slave trade and its many evils are long over and therefore not relevant to the modern world. However, undeniably, countless Black people continue to live with prejudice and economic hardship every day, which many link to the negative aftereffects of slavery and the slave trade. It is an integral and inseparable part of their heritage and identity.

Sometimes, the distinction between the perspectives of white

This engraving from the early 1800s depicts Africans participating in the slave trade, transporting their captives on the Congo River to a slave market where they were traded or purchased.

Americans and Europeans and Black Americans and Europeans is especially pronounced. The role of the African people in their own enslavement is one point of contention. It is a fact that Africans practiced slavery before European contact. In addition, African chiefs and local leaders aided white slave traders, selling other Africans to the Portuguese, Spanish, British, French, Dutch, and other white people who landed on their shores seeking cheap labor. In doing so, these leaders sought to maintain their power through goods and weapons obtained from Europeans. Some scholars use this practice as evidence that African Americans' own ancestors share responsibility for slavery in the Americas.

However, other scholars believe that it is a mistake to overemphasize this participation. First, the slavery of Africans before European arrival was not as harsh as the plantation slavery of the New World. Instead, enslaved Africans in Africa were treated more as servants, sometimes becoming like family members and earning freedom for themselves or their descendants over time. Also, the sale of Africans to Europeans was often not a completely voluntary act. Many African leaders took part in the transatlantic slave trade out of fear. In some cases, Europeans, who had more advanced weaponry than most Africans, threatened to declare war on those African peoples who refused to help them enslave other Africans. In addition, the European slave trade had changed the economics of Africa and made slavery the focal point. African American historian Anne C. Bailey explained:

> The slave business, promoted as it was by persistent European and American forces as well as African middlemen, had largely marginalized all other types of economic activity in [western Africa]. Within this context … under substantial pressure for slaves from [white] slave traders, Africans had few choices.[2]

Importantly, some scholars point out, it was not entire tribes or nations that decided local policy regarding the capture and sale of people. Rather, a few profit-seeking, immoral leaders made such decisions and forced their people to take part. "Here it is morally and factually important to make a distinction between collaborators among the people and the people themselves," wrote African American scholar Maulana Karenga. "Every people faced with conquest, oppression and destruction has had collaborators among them, but it is factually inaccurate and morally wrong and repulsive to indict [blame] a whole people for a holocaust which was imposed on them and was aided by collaborators."[3]

"A Great Tragedy"

Amid the ongoing debates about African involvement in the slave trade and the historical significance of the trade itself, modern observers agree on one point: This horrible chapter of human history must not be forgotten. It must continue to be taught in schools for future generations to try to understand. Books, articles, museums, documentary films, and websites must continue to examine and memorialize it for a public that is still endeavoring to comprehend its consequences.

In one of Africa's most widely spoken languages, Kiswahili (or Swahili), there is a term for the transatlantic slave trade: *Maafa*, which translates to "great tragedy." Many historians believe that the slave trade should be seen as an example of a holocaust due to the sheer number of deaths and abuses that occurred during the transportation and enslavement of millions of Africans. As such, it must remain in our history books and in our memories. As Anne C. Bailey described it, slavery and its evils should be kept in our consciousness "as a means of remembering so that we do not repeat the crimes of the past." In the end, she wrote, this period of history should "be remembered for the purpose of honoring those who did not survive it and addressing the problems and the challenges faced by those who did."[4]

Ghanaian artist Kwame Akoto-Bamfo created the art installation *Nkyinkyim* on display in the front of the National Memorial for Peace and Justice in Montgomery, Alabama. It reminds people of the horrors of the slave trade.

CHAPTER ONE

THE SPREAD OF SLAVERY

In 2008, the United Nations secretary-general, Ban Ki-moon, called the transatlantic slave trade "one of the greatest atrocities in history."[1] This atrocity took place over centuries and affected millions of people. According to the researchers of the Trans-Atlantic Slave Trade Database, more than 12.5 million Africans were shipped to the New World between 1525 and 1866. The overall number of transported people is even higher, though, since the practice of Europeans enslaving people from Africa began in the 1400s. In addition, many Africans were brought to the New World illegally and without record.

European slave traders became rich by treating African people as mere goods, forcibly taking them far from their homes and customs and selling them into a life of servitude. The slave trade relied on not only countries that enslaved people but also countries that bought goods that were produced through slave labor.

Slavery was not an invention of that time, though. It was an ancient institution, found in many places and among many cultures. It gained acceptance in Europe around the 1500s and 1600s, especially as many people began to see the opportunity to make a profit out of the labors of enslaved Africans. Countless others looked away while the atrocity occurred.

Slavery existed long before it came to the New World. When Roman armies captured new territories, it was common for them to enslave the conquered people, who are shown in this wall painting.

Slavery's Origins

It is natural to ask how European nations became involved in trafficking human beings on such a huge scale. After all, slavery was not very common in medieval Europe. For cheap labor, especially for agricultural workers, most wealthy people in that era relied on serfs. Mainly farmers who worked on a lord's land in exchange for protection, serfs were technically free but also closely dependent on landowners for a place to live, food to eat, and protection. As long as these highly dependent workers existed, slavery was not common in medieval Europe.

However, the slave-owning traditions of ancient times, which had culminated in the large-scale spread of slavery in ancient Rome, were not dead. In the early medieval centuries (roughly 500s and 600s CE), they remained alive and viable in various areas outside Europe—most notably among Arabs in the Middle East and North Africa. In the seventh and eighth centuries, following the rise of Islam in Arabia, Muslim armies spread outward and created an enormous empire. It stretched from what is now Iran and Iraq in the East, across North Africa, to southern Spain in the West. The Muslims maintained prosperous cities with impressive political and legal systems and centers of learning. Many upper-class members of that society supported their comfortable lifestyles partly through the exploitation of slave labor.

For the most part, these enslaved people came from sub-Saharan Africa. Traditional Islamic law did not allow Muslims to enslave each other, but Muslim merchants found a ready source of African captives in the lands lying just beyond the southern reaches of the Sahara. Some of these captives worked in homes and fields in the Muslim lands bordering the southern Mediterranean Sea. Other enslaved Africans were forced to convert to Islam and serve in Muslim armies. Historians estimate that a total of nearly 10 million sub-Saharan Africans were forced into slavery in Muslim societies between 600 and 1700. Accordingly, a large and sophisticated trans-Saharan slave network existed throughout medieval times and beyond. The transatlantic slave trade was, at least at the beginning, an outgrowth of this slave trafficking network long maintained by

PAST MEETS PRESENT: HUMAN TRAFFICKING

Many people today think slavery is an institution of the past. Sadly, this is not true. Modern slavery takes other forms that are illegal and less obvious than the transatlantic slave trade. Still, the victims suffer devastating consequences. It is estimated that millions of people around the world today are being exploited and enslaved.

In modern slavery, someone has control over another person in order to exploit them. They may threaten them with violence, money, or another sort of coercion. Sometimes the victims do not speak the language of the country they are in or are worried about being deported from the country if they are caught by authorities. Victims of modern slavery are forced to do whatever is asked of them. This could include a job like working in a factory or field, or it could include sexual exploitation. Victims do not think they can escape. They can come from any background and be of any age, but all are vulnerable in some way.

Human trafficking is the name for the act of coercing or trapping people into servitude. It is often a hidden crime, and sometimes the victims do not even recognize themselves as victims. Several organizations exist today to help people identify human trafficking and to encourage victims to seek help, such as the Blue Campaign in the United States and the Canadian Centre to End Human Trafficking.

Muslim merchants. Over time, Europeans began tapping into the sub-Saharan slave markets.

Enslaved for Sugar

In the 1300s, the Genoese, the inhabitants of the Italian kingdom of Genoa, began to see the economic potential of sugar plantations. Arab growers had been running such plantations in Egypt, Syria,

FROM THE SOURCE: GOBINEAU'S THE INEQUALITY OF HUMAN RACES

At first, overt racism played little part in the capture and sale of Africans in the transatlantic slave trade. Over time, however, many white people tried to justify their immoral and brutal buying and selling of other human beings by falsely insisting that Black people were racially, mentally, and morally inferior to white people, and therefore, it was acceptable to enslave them. Many Europeans came to accept some variation of the false argument expressed by a 19th-century French nobleman named Arthur de Gobineau in his book *The Inequality of Human Races*:

> *The negroid [Black] variety [of human] is the lowest, and stands at the foot of the ladder. The animal character, that appears in the shape of the pelvis, is stamped on the negro from birth, and foreshadows his destiny. His intellect will always move within a very narrow circle ... We come now to the white peoples. These are gifted with reflective energy, or rather with an energetic intelligence. They have a feeling for utility, but in a sense far wider and higher, more courageous and ideal ... a greater physical power, an extraordinary instinct for order.*[1]

This description may be shocking to read today, but many came to believe such absurd falsehoods, even attributing the ideas to science.

1. Arthur de Gobineau, *The Inequality of Human Races*, trans. Adrian Collins (London, UK: William Heinemann, 1915), pp. 205, 207, archive.org/stream/ inequalityofhuma00gobi#page/206/mode/2up.

and other areas of the Middle East for a few hundred years. The Genoese copied the Arab model, including importing enslaved Africans. By the early 1400s, Genoese growers and traders had begun to buy enslaved Africans through the trans-Saharan network to work on plantations on Cyprus and other Mediterranean islands.

These plantations were very successful financially, so it was not long before the chief European trade rivals of the Genoese—the Portuguese—began to set up their own sugar plantations. Like the Arabs and Genoese before them, the Portuguese saw that growing sugar was a complex, expensive proposition. Indeed, "sugar was a distinctive crop," historian Stuart B. Schwartz pointed out, adding:

> It called not only for good land and a particular climate but also for particularly heavy capital investment in buildings and equipment and a large labor force dedicated to continual and heavy activity during certain periods of the year ... Europeans engaged in few activities more complex than sugar production in the early modern period.[2]

In the mid-1400s, eager Portuguese investors and growers created large sugar plantations on the Cape Verde Islands, Madeira Islands, and Canary Islands, all lying off Africa's northwestern coast. Initially, they imported white European workers. Condemned prisoners, indentured servants, and orphans were among those who labored on these plantations. As time went on, however, the owners found it increasingly difficult to find the large numbers of workers they needed in Europe, which had relatively low supplies of cheap labor. The solution to this problem was to follow the Arab and Genoese lead by bringing in enslaved Africans.

The Portuguese found that importing enslaved Africans was not difficult. Adventurous Portuguese ship captains had recently been sailing south to explore Africa's western coast. Negotiating directly with local chiefs and leaders proved easier than tapping into the more time-consuming trans-Saharan network to the north. In the 1440s, Portuguese vessels carried more than 200 enslaved Africans to Lisbon—the capital of Portugal—and many of these laborers were then transported to plantations on the Madeira and Canary Islands. Shortly before 1500, Portuguese merchants and growers set up a thriving sugarcane industry on São Tomé, an island lying a few miles off the western African coast, and took advantage of African

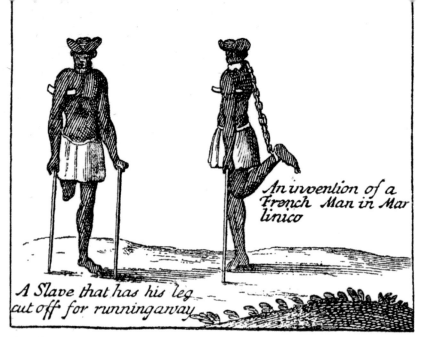

An invention of a French Man in Mar linico

A Slave that has his leg cut off for running away

This illustration from the 17th century shows how Portuguese enslavers punished enslaved people who ran away.

slave markets to supply the fields with cheap labor.

The first Africans brought to Portugal in the mid-1400s became either household servants or laborers on sugar plantations. A Portuguese noble of that era, Gomes Eanes de Zurara, described his impression of some of these enslaved people in a book about the western African country of Guinea:

> They never more tried to fly [flee], but rather in time forgot all about their own country, as soon as they began to taste the good things of this one … They were very loyal and obedient servants, without malice … After they began to use clothing they were for the most part very fond of display, so that they took great delight in robes of showy colours, and such was their love of finery, that they picked up the rags that fell from the coats of other people of the country and sewed them on to their [own] garments.[3]

Plantations in the Americas

The successful São Tomé plantation became the chief model for the European sugar plantations that sprang up in the recently

HISTORY HAPPENED HERE: SÃO TOMÉ

The island of São Tomé is located on the equator in the Gulf of Guinea, off the coast of West Africa. It was uninhabited until discovered by the Portuguese in 1470, who imported settlers as well as enslaved Africans to set up a plantation economy in the 1490s. It became a source of wealth for the Portuguese. However, hundreds of enslaved people who worked on the island escaped to the mountains, creating their own society. Under the leadership of a man named Amador, they tried to take over the island in 1595 but were defeated by the Portuguese.

The island continued to be a source of sugar and coffee, thanks to its rich soil. At one point, it was also the world's leading exporter of cocoa. Slavery's grip held on to the island for a long time. Slavery was finally abolished there in 1875. The island became independent of Portugal in 1975.

colonized Americas in the early 1500s. At first, the Portuguese and Spanish dominated both colonization and the slave trade in the New World. The 1494 Treaty of Tordesillas between the two nations gave Portugal virtual control of the western African region and Brazil, while Spain acquired control of Central America and the Caribbean region.

The Spanish were the first to set up sugar plantations in the Americas, with an operation on the island of Hispaniola, east of Cuba, by 1502. Such outposts became known as exploitation colonies, or tropical dependencies. The growers concentrated on turning out large quantities of cash crops—not only sugarcane, but also spices and cotton. In order to make a decent profit, all these crops required large numbers of inexpensive workers. At the beginning, the Spanish plantations did not do as well as their owners had expected. First, Spanish investors and governors increasingly shifted

This 1595 copper engraving shows enslaved people working hard on a sugar plantation on Hispaniola.

their resources into looking for gold and other valuables in Mexico, rather than supporting agriculture. Second, Spanish growers exploited the existing Native populations for cheap labor rather than importing large numbers of Black Africans; this approach proved unproductive because the Native American workers quickly died out or became too few to turn a profit. On Hispaniola, for example, the Spanish had worked to death, murdered, or passed deadly diseases on to nearly all of that island's native inhabitants by the 1600s.

To replace those who had died, the Spanish turned to two sources—cheap white European laborers and enslaved Africans. The white laborers—including convicts, war prisoners, orphans, and indentured servants—had been exploited for generations in Europe and elsewhere. However, it had become more and more expensive to import them from Europe. Also, increasing social pressures demanded a shift from exploitation of white labor to exploitation of Black labor, especially from the early 1600s on. Part of the reason

THEY MADE HISTORY: CHRISTOPHER COLUMBUS

Christopher Columbus is widely known as the man who opened the Americas to European exploration. He did this accidentally with his voyage of 1492, an endeavor to locate a western route to Asia. Born in Genoa, Italy, in 1451 as Cristoforo Colombo, Columbus moved to Portugal in 1476. It was there that he began to plan to find a western route to Asia in order to make trade easier. However, the Portuguese king would not finance Columbus's trip, so he appealed to the Spanish king and queen. They agreed, providing Columbus with three ships.

On August 3, 1492, the voyage began, reaching the Bahamas, east of Florida, in October. Columbus mistakenly believed he had reached the East Indies in Asia. The expedition went on to Cuba and then the island of Hispaniola (today's Haiti and Dominican Republic). He returned to Spain with parrots, plants, gold, cloth, and several Native Americans. Columbus made return voyages to the islands. After one, he brought 500 Taino people from Hispaniola to Spain, intending to enslave them. Just 300 survived the trip. Eventually, enslaving indigenous peoples became common. Columbus died in 1506, still thinking he had found a way to Asia.

Christopher Columbus enslaved some of the indigenous people he encountered on his voyages to the Americas.

enslaved Africans emerged as the Europeans' first choice for workers was that they seemed different. Not only were they from a distant continent, their skin color and traditions were different from Spanish or Portuguese cultural practices. This made it easier for slave traders to treat Black people as little more than animals or products to be sold.

Over time, the Spanish increased their importation of African laborers, which increased the profitability of their exploitation colonies. Throughout the 1500s and well into the 1600s, they bought enslaved Africans from Portuguese traders, who still controlled most of the West African markets. After 1640, when Spain and Portugal became enemies, the Spanish turned to the Dutch, French, and eventually the British for shipments of Africans. All those countries were happy to supply them.

In the same years that the Spanish plantations were experiencing mixed success, the Portuguese created an extremely profitable plantation system in Brazil. The Brazilian sugar plantations used enslaved people early on, following the São Tomé model. Some attempts were made to exploit the local Native populations, but similarly to the Spanish, these efforts proved mostly fruitless. The earliest voyage recorded of African captives crossing the Atlantic to Brazil was in 1538, and by 1600, almost all the laborers on the Brazilian plantations were Black workers. Enslaved Africans were also imported to work in Portuguese gold mines in central Brazil and on coffee plantations in the southern part of the country.

Meanwhile, other Europeans began competing with the Spanish and Portuguese. In 1627, the British opened their first sugar plantation on the island of Barbados. By 1643—only 16 years later—they had imported thousands of Africans to the colony. By the 1660s, more than 40,000 Black people lived and worked on Barbados, almost twice the number of white colonists.

British, Dutch, and other European merchants also established successful exploitation colonies on the Caribbean islands of Jamaica, St. Croix, and Guadeloupe. Particularly profitable was the French Caribbean colony of Saint-Domingue on Hispaniola. When French planters took control of the island from Spain in the late 1600s, they immediately began exploiting the enslaved Black people (some of whom had been imported earlier by the Spanish) as a workforce. By the late 1700s, the colony supported around 40,000 white people of French ancestry, 28,000 free Black and mixed-race people, and a staggering 450,000 enslaved Black laborers.

Triangular Trade

The Caribbean, Brazilian, and other American colonies that came to exploit large numbers of enslaved Africans also took advantage of the very profitable commercial network that developed in the 1500s and 1600s in the Atlantic region. It became known as the triangular trade because it featured three primary legs of profitable production. The first leg of the triangle consisted of the export of goods from Europe to Africa. In deals struck with African leaders who owned or could capture large numbers of people, European merchants swapped these goods for enslaved Africans.

The second leg of the Atlantic triangular trade was the sale of the enslaved Africans in the Americas. This sale turned a profit for the slave traders. It also allowed the buyers—the plantation owners— to turn their own profits afterward, because the enslaved people they purchased were inexpensive to feed and clothe. They were also cheap enough to make it viable to regularly replace agricultural laborers who died of overwork or harsh living conditions. At the same time, enslaved people who worked in the household, who had less backbreaking jobs, could produce children, leading to two, three, or more workers for each one bought from a slave trader.

The third and final leg of the triangular trade was the sale of goods produced by the enslaved people in American colonies to markets in Europe. Sugar, cotton, tobacco, molasses, rum, spices, and other goods turned out by American plantations and farms flowed into Europe, contributing still more profits for enterprising traders. With this profit, merchants bought the necessary trade goods to use in Africa, in the first leg of the next three-way trading cycle. This continued for centuries.

Such large-scale mercantile operations particularly benefited big investors. As a rule, only wealthy traders—those who could build

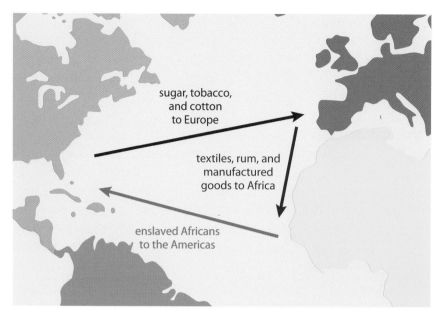

sugar, tobacco,
and cotton
to Europe

textiles, rum, and
manufactured
goods to Africa

enslaved Africans
to the Americas

In reality, the triangular trade was more complicated than just three routes, but the shape represents the basic profit cycle rooted in slavery.

and maintain their own fleets of ships—could afford to take an occasional serious loss and still manage to keep putting money into new enslaving ventures. Because the extremely wealthy could split up their operations among several ships, which helped them reduce the impact of any one loss, they were able to reap unprecedented profits without taking on as much risk. On the other hand, smaller businesses and investors found it difficult to make such large gains—and they also shouldered a lot more risk. A merchant with only one ship, for example, could have his fortunes ruined by a single storm at sea.

Enter England

Portugal may have been one of the early leaders of the Atlantic slave trade, but England became the dominant country on the slave-trading routes from the late 1600s to 1807, when the slave trade was abolished in that nation and its colonies. Portuguese and British ships transported an estimated 70 percent of all enslaved Africans to the Americas, and of these, 3.1 million Africans were taken to the British colonies. Professor James Walvin, a transatlantic slave trade historian, stated, "The British have always seen slavery as an American institution, but in reality, all the Africans that became American slaves were taken to the continent by British ships. The British were absolutely central and seminal to the entire system."[4]

England used these enslaved people to make their colonies on the eastern coast of North America financially successful. At first, these British colonies, which included Virginia, the Carolinas, and Georgia, needed and used few enslaved Africans. However, slavery was a part of every British colony by the 1700s, and not only the wealthy people bought enslaved people. Some who would be considered middle class had enslaved laborers, renting them out to others who needed their labor. The institution became common and deeply rooted in colonial America, eventually requiring a civil war to extract it completely from the United States.

How You See History

1. What does the widespread practice of slavery, from ancient Rome to colonial America, reveal about the different cultures that relied on it?

2. Do you think enslaved people at that time would agree with Gomes Eanes de Zurara's description of them? Why or why not?

3. Why do you think Christopher Columbus's connection with slavery is not as widely known as his voyage to the Americas?

COLONIAL LABOR

England was late to the transatlantic slave trade compared to some other European countries. In fact, the British colonies of North America were among the last colonies in that part of the world to participate in the slave trade. In the 1600s, England was determined to establish successful colonies on the North American continent. The focus was on settling enduring communities with families, not just turning a profit with large-scale plantations as some European countries were doing in other regions of the Americas. Many of the British settlers had moved to North America to escape prejudice and seek new opportunities. The search for great wealth was not necessarily a factor for many. The first permanent British colony was Jamestown, Virginia, established in 1607. Eventually, other groups also had success founding colonies on the eastern coast of the continent.

However, the great amount of work that came with each colony's continued growth became apparent, particularly as success was tied to the agricultural products, called cash crops, that could be cultivated and sold in Europe. Tobacco in particular was found to grow well in Virginia and was greatly desired by Europeans. Other crops, such as rice and indigo, were also sought-after exports. To increase profits, the colonists needed an influx of laborers, particularly in

Robert Milligan, whose statue was removed from London in 2020 for his ties to the slave trade, owned two sugar plantations and more than 500 enslaved people in Jamaica.

HISTORY HAPPENED HERE: LIVERPOOL AND THE INTERNATIONAL SLAVERY MUSEUM

From the mid-1700s to 1807, Liverpool, England, was the busiest port involved in the slave trade in all of Europe. Between 1695 and 1807, about 5,300 ships set sail from Liverpool for Africa. These ships later carried about 1.5 million enslaved Africans to the Americas. The next busiest slave port was London with 3,100 vessels.

Liverpool was chosen as the site for the world's only museum dedicated to the history of the transatlantic slave trade. Called the International Slavery Museum, it opened in 2007, which was the 200th anniversary of the abolition of the British slave trade. This museum seeks to inform visitors of the terrible ordeal faced by enslaved people of the past as well as to discuss slavery's impact on the world today.

Exhibits include a display highlighting West African cultural artifacts before the transatlantic slave trade as well

the southern British colonies where cash crops grew well. At first, indentured servants from Europe as well as Native people fit this demand. This labor system was not always fair. Native Americans, for example, were often paid poorly. Many indentured European workers did not live long enough to pay off their debt in the harsh conditions of the New World. Indentured servants began to seem expensive to landowners who needed labor. They also did not work for their entire lifetime. In addition, fewer people were willing to submit to the contract for this kind of work. The African slave trade became more attractive to those seeking to increase their profits with a cheaper source of labor.

About 15,000 Africans had reached the British colonies by the 1690s. In the first two decades of the 1700s, about 26,000 enslaved Africans were brought to the colonies. Nearly 37,000 more landed

These masks are on display at the International Slavery Museum, exhibiting the rich cultural history of West Africans.

as a film that shows visitors what the frightening voyage to the Americas may have been like for enslaved Africans. More than 3.5 million people have visited the museum since its opening.

in the 1720s. In the 1730s, about 62,000 Africans were brought in as laborers. After that, an average of 35,000 Africans arrived in the colonies in each decade until the American Revolution in the 1770s. British merchants with dealings in slavery became rich.

During this time, the treatment of enslaved people altered drastically. At first, they were treated more as indentured servants, some even gaining freedom after a time. However, as more enslaved Africans arrived, the worse their treatment at the hands of their enslavers and society in general became. Racism gained a foothold in every British colony and wound its way into colonial culture.

Looking for Laborers

When tobacco growers in Virginia and elsewhere in colonial America recognized the need for increased amounts of cheap labor, they first considered exploiting the local Native Americans. However, it did not take long for the white colonists to realize that the Native Americans were going to be difficult to enslave. The colonists "were outnumbered," American historian Howard Zinn pointed out, "and while, with superior firearms, they could massacre Indians, they would face massacre in return. They could not capture them and keep them enslaved; the Indians were tough, resourceful, defiant, and at home in the woods, as the transplanted Englishmen were not."[1]

Moreover, superior English technology, including firearms and metal plows, did not prove effective in forcing the Native Americans to work on white farms. "If you were a colonist," historian Edmund Morgan explained,

> you knew that your technology was superior to the Indians' … But your superior technology had proved insufficient to extract anything. The Indians, keeping to themselves, laughed at your superior methods and lived from the land more abundantly and with less labor than you did … So you killed the Indians, tortured them, burned their villages, burned their cornfields. It proved your superiority, in spite of your failures … But you still did not grow much corn.[2]

It soon became clear that acquiring and using enslaved Africans would be considerably easier than enslaving large numbers of Native Americans. First, the colonists did not have to go out and capture the Africans, who came to the colonies already in chains. Also, to the Africans, the North American colonies were a frightening new land, a strange region filled with unknown dangers. Even if they escaped their white enslavers, they would be at the mercy of the Native Americans, who knew the area and were armed with hatchets, bows, knives, and other weapons. It was unlikely, therefore, that those who were enslaved would risk trying to escape the colonial farms on which they worked.

These were among the reasons that some colonists in Jamestown, Virginia, bought around 20 Africans from a Dutch slave trader in 1619. These enslaved Africans were the first to arrive in the British colonies that would become the United States. Almost every year thereafter, more Africans arrived in the British colonies. At first, the

PAST MEETS PRESENT: GHANA'S YEAR OF RETURN

To mark 400 years since the first slave ship arrived in the American colonies and the long legacy of Africans being uprooted from their homeland, the country of Ghana began an initiative in 2019 called "The Year of Return." The West African nation was a central hub in the transatlantic slave trade. The campaign, begun by Ghanian president Nana Akufo-Addo, called for African Americans to visit Ghana to explore their culture, connect with the experiences of their ancestors, invest in the country's industries, or even permanently move to Ghana. It was also a celebration of the resilience of the African people who suffered from the slave trade, hoping to link their descendants with the culture that was stolen from them so many years ago. The Year of Return proved to be a boost to Ghana's economy and tourism industry. It attracted hundreds of thousands of visitors, including celebrities such as model Naomi Campbell, actor Idris Elba, comedian Steve Harvey, and rapper Cardi B.

slave trade made little impact in the colonies because the number of enslaved Africans remained relatively low. This was partly because the British distrusted people who were foreign-born.

Additionally, indentured servants—who were exclusively white Europeans—were still both popular and preferable in the colonies. Indentured servants were people who agreed to work for a certain amount of time, often five years, in exchange for someone to pay their fare for transportation across the ocean and room and board while working off their debt. When indentured servants paid their debt, part of the agreement often required that the landowner give them something to get them started on their new life, such as money or land. In general, the concept behind indentured servitude was that the landowners temporarily owned the servants' labor but did not own the servants themselves. Indentured servants already spoke the English language, which made them preferable to their Native American and African competition. Because their service was voluntary, they were not likely to attempt escape. Finally, indentured servants could eventually be expected to assimilate into mainstream society as full members.

For these reasons, white indentured servants remained the labor-intensive backbone of large colonial farms in the early 17th century. The number of imported Africans remained fairly low. In 1625, for example, 6 years after the first enslaved Africans had arrived in Virginia, that colony's census listed fewer than 30 Black residents. As late as the mid-1650s, only a few hundred Black people lived in the colonies of Virginia and Maryland combined.

Freedoms of Early Africans

These few Africans worked alongside indentured servants and other poor white laborers. Typically, both white and Black workers put in the same number of hours in an average day or average week. On many farms in Virginia and nearby colonies, Black and white laborers shared the same sleeping areas, ate the same food, and on occasion, had children together. The few Africans scattered around the colonies were viewed by poor whites as fellow workers who did not like their jobs—rather than as inferiors. Overt racism based on skin color had not yet become a significant factor in the social situation of enslaved Black people in the British colonies in North America.

It is therefore not surprising that, at first, some Africans gained their freedom just as white indentured servants did. In 1668, in Virginia's Northampton County, for instance, there were around 40 Africans who had earned their freedom in some way. Some had borrowed money from their enslavers and purchased their freedom with it. Once free, the Africans got a paying job and paid back that debt over time. A few enslaved people petitioned local courts to obtain their freedom. Typically, they argued that, like white indentured servants, they had worked a number of years faithfully and to their enslavers' financial benefit; it was, therefore, only fair and fitting that the term of service should entitle them to eventual freedom. Still other Black colonists enjoyed freedom because they came from mixed marriages. When a white man married an enslaved Black woman, their children were legally free.

The practice of an enslaved person being able to "buy" their freedom like an indentured servant persisted in some places. This document from 1794 outlines how a formerly enslaved person in Pennsylvania would work for the man who paid for his freedom for a period of time.

In addition to having the legal right to borrow money, petition the courts, and gain their freedom, Black residents in early colonial times were sometimes able to own land. Surviving evidence from Virginia suggests that around a dozen free Black residents owned their own farms. Most of these landowners owned livestock, and the wealthiest had their own rosters of enslaved people. The fact that some enslaved Black people gained their freedom reveals an important aspect of the transatlantic slave trade in early colonial America: It was not yet a significant economic force in the colonies. As long as there were enough white laborers in North America, the transatlantic trade in Africans remained centered far to the south in the exploitation colonies of the Caribbean and Central and South America.

The Growth of the Slave Trade

This type of slavery, which allowed the enslaved some hope of freedom, was not destined to persist. The late 1600s and early 1700s witnessed an enormous increase in the number of enslaved Africans shipped to colonial America. One reason for this increase was

THEY MADE HISTORY: PHILLIS WHEATLEY

Although all Africans who became unwillingly caught up in the transatlantic slave trade were initially treated like mere products rather than human beings, a few were fortunate enough to fall in with kind, socially progressive families. This was the case for Phillis Wheatley, an enslaved African woman who became renowned for her poetry. Kidnapped from her village in West Africa, she landed in Boston, Massachusetts, in 1761, when she was eight years old. At a slave auction, a local merchant named John Wheatley purchased

Phillis Wheatley was the first African American—and one of the first women—to publish a book in the American colonies.

a major reduction in the number of white indentured servants available from Europe. Economic prosperity was rapidly expanding in England, in part because of the success of the triangular trading system and British plantations on Barbados and other exploitation colonies. As a result, more lower-class British workers were able to find jobs, either in their homeland or abroad, so they felt no need to sign themselves into servitude. Other factors reducing the number of indentured servants included a declining birth rate in England and the creation of many construction jobs following the Great Fire of London in 1666. With fewer indentured servants arriving in the colonies, landowners began buying more enslaved Africans. The dramatic turnaround can be seen in surviving records from her as a personal maid to his wife. The couple and their daughter tutored Phillis in English, Latin, Greek, geography, history, and other academic subjects. With the family's help, Phillis published her first poem in 1767, when she was just 14. In 1773, the Wheatleys sent Phillis to London, where she published *Poems on Various Subjects, Religious and Moral*. In one of the poems in this collection, she talks of her background, when she was stolen from Africa:

> I, young in life, by seeming cruel fate
> Was snatch'd from Afric's fancy'd happy seat:
> What pangs excruciating must molest,
> What sorrows labour in my parent's breast?
> Steel'd was that soul and by no misery mov'd
> That from a father seiz'd his babe belov'd:
> Such, such my case. And can I then but pray
> Others may never feel tyrannic sway?[1]

On returning to Boston, Phillis Wheatley received her freedom.

1. Phillis Wheatley, "To the Right Honorable William, Earl of Dartmouth," Poetry Foundation, www.poetryfoundation.org/poems/47706/to-the-right-honorable-william-earl-of-dartmouth (accessed May 13, 2020).

Virginia. In most areas of that colony, enslaved people replaced indentured servants almost entirely as workers for the prosperous agriculture merchants.

Dutch, French, Portuguese, and other slave traders were more than happy to meet the new demands for enslaved Africans in England's American colonies. At first, the biggest concentration of new Africans was in the coastal colonies of Virginia and Maryland. Virginia's census records indicate that in 1670, the colony had about 2,000 Black people, roughly 6 percent of the overall population of 35,000. By 1700, there were 16,000 Black people in Virginia, making up more than 25 percent of the population of 58,000. By 1760, the colony had about 140,000 Black people, accounting for more than 40 percent of the overall population of 340,000. Moreover, during these same years, the number of enslaved Black laborers increased in every British colony, especially those south of Maryland.

In New York, Massachusetts, and other northern colonies, however, no significant plantation economy developed, so there was far less need for importing enslaved Africans. Nevertheless, some northerners did use enslaved Africans for small-scale farming or manufacturing. By 1750, Massachusetts had about 4,000 enslaved Africans out of a total population of around 190,000, and in 1760, Rhode Island had about 3,500 out of its total population of about 45,000.

One important reason that so many American colonists could afford to buy large numbers of enslaved Africans was that the price per person decreased noticeably in the late 1600s and early 1700s. This drop in price was mostly because of a dramatic increase in England's participation and share in the entire triangular trading process, especially the transatlantic slave leg. Portugal, Spain, the Netherlands, and France had long dominated the trade, but in 1672, the British-run Royal African Company began shipping enslaved people directly from West Africa to colonial America, as well as to England's Caribbean colonies. The company quickly acquired what amounted to a monopoly in the slave markets of these colonies by offering special deals to fellow Englishmen.

As one scholar wrote, in a market in which the Portuguese and Dutch were

An Account of the Number of Negroes delivered in to the Islands of Barbadoes, Jamaica, and Antego, from the Year 1698 to 1708. since the Trade was Opened, taken from the Accounts sent from the respective Governours of those Islands to the Lords Commissioners of Trade, whereby it appears the African Trade is encreas'd to four times more since its being laid Open, than it was under an Exclusive Company.

Between what Years deliver'd.	N°. of Negroes delivered into Barbados.	Number delivered into Jamaica.	Number delivered into Antego.
Between the 8 April, 1698			
To April 1699	3436		
To April 1700	3080		
To 5 ditto 1701	4311		
To 10 ditto 1702	9213		
To 31 Mar. 1703	4561		
To 5 April 1704	1876		
To 2d. ditto 1705	3219		
To 5 ditto 1706	1875		
To 12 May 1707	2730		
To 29 April 1708	1018		
Between 29 Sept. - - 1698 and 29 Decemb. 1698		1273	
Between 7 April - - 1699 and 28 March 1700		5766	
From 28 Mar.to 3 Apr. 1701		6668	
3 Apr. 1701.to 20 dit. 1702		8505	
20 dit. 1702 to 12 dit. 1703		2238	
12 dit.1703 to 18 dit. 1704		2711	
18 dit.1704 to 24 dit. 1705		3421	
24 dit.1705 to 27 dit. 1706		5462	
27 dit.1706 to 22 dit. 1707		2122	
22 dit.1707 to 26 dit. 1708		6623	
To June 1708		187	
1698			18
June 1699			212
Between June - - 1700 and 24 April 1701			364
Between 24 April - 1701 and 30 March 1702			2395
To April 1703			1670
To Nov. 1704			1551
To 1705			569
To 1706			530
To 1707			114
	35409	44376	7123

Besides which there are 7 Separate Ships named in the foregoing List for Antego, but not the Number of Negroes, so we may well compute them at 1200 more, which arriv'd between 1699 and 1700.

This image shows a record of the numbers of Africans delivered to the islands of Barbados, Jamaica, and Antigua from 1698 to 1708.

charging 25 British pounds for an enslaved African, the Royal African Company

> *announced that if persons would contract to receive whole cargoes [of Africans] upon their arrival [in the Americas] and to accept all slaves between twelve and forty years of age who were able to go over the ship's side unaided they would be supplied at a rate of £15 [15 pounds] per head in Barbados … £17 in Jamaica, and £18 in Virginia.*[3]

Tightening Control

As a result of these changes, in the first two decades of the 18th century, more than twice as many Africans arrived in colonial America as had been transported there in the entire previous century. Moreover, the attitudes of white colonists toward Black workers changed. No longer did lower-class white workers see Black laborers as fellow human beings sharing their fate. The increasing number of Africans, especially in the southern colonies, made them seem more threatening. Both white slaveholders and white workers increasingly worried not only about uprisings but also about freed Black people marrying white people and taking jobs from white workers.

In fear, white society clamped down on its former relatively lenient social and legal treatment of Black people. To start, Africans who arrived on slave ships could no longer look forward to the possibility of earning their freedom. More and more, white people treated the Africans as a product to be exploited and abused, which had the effect of dehumanizing Black people more thoroughly than ever before. Newspaper ads for newly arrived Africans typically depicted them as less than human. An ad in the June 6, 1763, issue of the *Newport Gazette* reads as if newly arrived Africans were a kind of farm animal:

> *On Thursday last arrived from the coast of Africa, the brig Royal Charlotte with a parcel of extremely fine, healthy, well limb'd [strong] Gold Coast slaves, men, women, boys and girls. Gentlemen in town and country have now an opportunity to furnish*

FROM THE SOURCE: SLAVE CODES

In the late 1600s and early 1700s, various British colonies passed comprehensive legal codes (rules and regulations) covering many different aspects of the treatment and control of enslaved Black people in white society. Enacted in 1740 after a failed slave rebellion, South Carolina's sweeping slave code, named "An Act for the Better Ordering and Governing Negroes and Other Slaves in This Province," decreed:

For the better keeping slaves in due order and subjection ... no person whatsoever shall permit or suffer [allow] any slave under his or their care or management, and who lives or is employed in Charlestown [Charleston], or any other town in this Province, to go out of the limits of the said town, or any such slave who lives in the country, to go out of the plantation to which such slave belongs, or in which plantation such slave is usually employed, without a letter ... or a ticket ... Without such letter or ticket as aforesaid, or without a white person in his company, [the enslaved person] shall be punished with whipping on the bare back, not exceeding twenty lashes.[1]

1. "An Act for the Better Ordering and Governing Negroes and Other Slaves in This Province," Teaching American History in South Carolina Project, digital. scetv.org/teachingAmerhistory/pdfs/Transciptionof1740SlaveCodes.pdf (accessed June 9, 2020).

themselves with such [enslaved people] as will suit them. They [the Africans] are to be seen on the vessel at Taylor's wharf.[4]

One way that white colonists ensured that all people shipped in from Africa would be kept in a state of permanent slavery was to severely tighten local laws pertaining to Black people. For example, before the late 1600s, Virginia had considered offspring of a white father and Black mother to be free. As racism spread, a new law erased this legal standard. All children born in the colony were now viewed as either enslaved or free based solely on the race of the mother. Furthermore, another new law stated that any "white man or woman being free [who] shall intermarry with a negro, mulatto [mixed-race person], or Indian"[5] was to be banished from the colony.

The Rise of Racism

The expansion of the slave trade and continuing dehumanizing of enslaved Africans led to an overall increase in racism. Racism is the belief that one race is superior or inferior to another. By claiming that white people were superior to Black people, enslavers had created a false justification of the slave trade. Denying that Africans were as human as themselves and as worthy of respect allowed them to disregard the evils of the practice of slavery. Further, Black people were all grouped into one category based on the color of their skin, disregarding that they had come from many different regions and cultures. Reducing them to "property" meant there was little need to empathize with their situation.

Many historians and sociologists agree that the development of racism in the New World—though it has always existed between groups around the globe to some extent—was key to institutionalizing slavery, making it an accepted structure of society. Even as the Founding Fathers of the United States were mulling over the idea of liberty from Great Britain, the rights of the individual, and equality among Americans, most excluded enslaved people from this discussion entirely. Slavery was so deeply rooted in colonial life that it was permanently ingrained in the culture and politics of America even after the colonies became independent from Britain.

How You See History

1. How did the early freedoms held by the first enslaved people in the colonies threaten the institution of slavery?

2. How did attitudes about enslaved Africans change over time in the British colonies? Why did this happen?

3. Do you think slavery could have expanded as it did without the spread of racism? Why or why not?

CHAPTER THREE

CAPTIVE IN AFRICA

The same incomplete records that make it challenging to know exactly how many Africans were forced into slavery also make it difficult to know what parts of Africa these people came from. However, researchers think about half came from what are today the countries of Senegal, Gambia, Guinea-Bissau, Mali, Angola, the Republic of the Congo, the Democratic Republic of the Congo, and Gabon. The other half likely came from the West African nations of Ghana, Benin, Togo, and Ivory Coast, as well as parts of Nigeria and Cameroon.

Just as these nations today are diverse in their cultures, the Africans taken from them over the centuries were of different ethnicities, language groups, and traditions. In fact, European enslavers preferred a mix of people from different backgrounds so they would be less likely to band together against their enslavement. They thought that it was a way to strip people of their identities, replacing them with the idea that they were property with one purpose: to please their enslavers. Enslaved Africans were usually sent to the Americas with nothing that could remind them of home, sometimes not even clothing. Only their memories bound them to their past.

Millions of Africans were victims in the transatlantic slave trade, but some also participated in it. Slavery was a part of life on the African continent, a part which slave traders found easy to exploit

Today, the continent of Africa is home to more than 50 nations and thousands of ethnic groups.

THEY MADE HISTORY: AYUBA SULEIMAN DIALLO

In the 1700s, at the height of the slave trade, so many Africans were carelessly captured and sold into slavery that, on occasion, some of the slave traders themselves ended up in bondage. This was what happened to Ayuba Suleiman Diallo, also known as Job Ben Solomon. Born about 1701 in the nation of Futa Toro (now Senegal), Diallo was a well-educated Muslim merchant who sometimes dealt in slavery. Around 1731, Diallo and his assistants were captured by Africans, who sold them to a British slave trader. Diallo soon found himself doing hard labor on a tobacco plantation in Maryland.

After attempting to escape, he was jailed for a time. While in prison, he met a man named Thomas Bluett, who was impressed with Diallo's level of education. Though Diallo was returned to the plantation, he wrote a letter to his father that was intercepted by the head of the British Royal African Company. Recognizing that Diallo was different from most enslaved Africans, the official purchased his freedom. Diallo was then taken to England, where some wealthy men, including Bluett, gave him money after learning of his fears that he would be sold back into slavery or ransomed. He used the money to return to Africa in 1734, where he worked for the Royal African Company in the slave trade until his death in 1773. Thomas Bluett wrote Diallo's memoirs, which became a popular slave narrative. It was titled *Some Memoirs of the Life of Job, the Son of Solomon, the High Priest of Boonda in Africa; Who Was a Slave About Two Years in Maryland; and Afterwards Being Brought to England, Was Set Free, and Sent to His Native Land in the Year 1734.*

for their own gain. Understanding the systems of slavery in Africa and how those were exploited is a crucial part of understanding the history of the transatlantic slave trade.

Slavery in Africa

Most nations and ethnic groups of West Africa, in one way or another, played a role in the transatlantic slave trade. Africans regularly captured and sold other Africans, either to neighboring nations or to white slave traders. Slavery was an age-old institution that had existed in West Africa long before white slave traders arrived.

The most common route into slavery in Africa, both before and after the arrival of the white slave traders, was to be captured in war. Once the European demand for Africans was established, it was not unusual for one African group to go to war with another primarily to obtain captives that could be sold to the white slave traders. In other cases, members of one African group kidnapped residents of neighboring nations or villages. Such raids sometimes provoked wars of revenge, which produced still more captives for one side or the other. Typically, the aggressors marched the captives to the coast, where the Europeans had constructed large forts or other structures to hold people awaiting trade.

It is important to emphasize that even though the people of West Africa practiced slavery, there were significant differences between the African and European versions of the institution. Enslaved people in Africa were similar in many ways to European indentured servants. They received small wages for their labors and had the option of eventually gaining their freedom. According to John Newton, a British slave trader who later became an abolitionist:

> The state of Slavery, among these wild barbarous people, as we esteem [view] them, is much milder than in our colonies. For as, on the one hand, they have no land in high cultivation, like our West-India [Caribbean] plantations, and therefore no call for that excessive, unintermitted [nonstop] labour, which exhausts our Slaves; so, on the other hand, no man is permitted to draw blood, even from a Slave. If he does, he is liable to a strict inquisition [investigation].[1]

Enslaved Africans worked as artisans as well as menial laborers and quite often became trusted members of families and respected members of their communities. They were not often abused physically and mentally for years on end, as they were in the New World.

HISTORY HAPPENED HERE: CAPE COAST CASTLE

Cape Coast Castle is located in Cape Coast, Ghana, in West Africa. It once served as a prison fort that held Africans who would be transported to the Americas by slave ships. The structure, one of about 40 such "slave castles" on the African coast, was first built by the Swedish Africa Company in the 1600s but switched possession several times, at different points claimed by the Danish, Dutch, and British. The building was altered over the years to increase its holding capacity.

One especially dark reminder of Cape Coast Castle's role in history is called the "Door of No Return." Through this door, thousands of people walked from imprisonment in the windowless dungeons, also called slave holes, to the ships that would take them to a lifetime of servitude on another continent. U.S. president Barack Obama visited Cape Coast Castle in 2009 and remarked that the structure "reminds us of the capacity of human beings to commit great evil."[1]

1. Quoted in Michael Scherer, "Obama's Statement at Cape Coast Castle," Time.com, July 11, 2009, swampland.time.com/2009/07/11/obamas-statement-at-cape-coast-castle/.

As many as 1,500 Africans were kept in the suffocating dungeons of Cape Coast Castle at one time.

Europeans in Africa

The transition from African slavery to European slavery, which was far more harsh and inhumane, was therefore a great shock to those Africans who were taken to the coast and sold to white traders. Neither the Europeans nor the African slave runners they dealt with cared that the people sold were about to enter a more brutal system. All the white traders cared about was acquiring as many Africans as they could for the cheapest prices possible. This would increase profit margins for their supervisors, which led to increased salaries or bonuses. The entire transatlantic slave trading system was built on foundations of economic success.

During negotiations, the European agents, as a rule, treated their African counterparts with contempt. The general white view was that the Africans, no matter how wealthy and powerful they might be in their own nations, were "savages" who were inferior to European whites in every way. A British slave trader named Nicholas Owen stated in his journal, "These people that goes [go] by the names of kings and princes are only so in title. Their substance consists of nothing more than a lace hat, a gown and silver-headed cane … to distinguish them from the rest of the negros [Black people]."[2]

Nevertheless, this racist disapproval for the natives had to be tempered with a healthy respect for their military skills and their ability to defend their land. Modern depictions of European enslavers heading inland, attacking native villages, and dragging hundreds of captives to the coast are largely fictional. Such raids did occur occasionally in certain areas where and when the situation allowed. For the most part, though, the local African societies were in full control of their territories, including the coastal regions.

Historians have pointed out that as the African leaders realized that the Europeans were not peaceful explorers, they began to secure their homeland as much as possible. Though they lacked the weaponry of their white counterparts, the Africans were experts in the lay of their land. They had spent generations hunting, surviving, and building societies around their forests and rivers, so any inland fighting would have left the Europeans at a major tactical disadvantage. Moreover, the earliest expeditions from Europe to Africa were extremely difficult; sailors were exhausted after the lengthy journey,

One recorded method of Europeans enslaving Africans involved setting fire to their villages and capturing them as they fled.

and few of them had combat experience. Most wanted to get their pay and get on with their jobs—and that rarely included fighting the native people in doomed land battles.

Another powerful deterrent to white slave traders venturing inland was fear of catching exotic diseases, including malaria, which could be fatal. As a result, even though the Europeans almost always had superior weapons, there were few armed conflicts between white and Black slave traders on Africa's coast.

The March to the Coast

The first time that most captured Africans saw a white person was when they arrived on the Atlantic coast after a forced march from whichever region of Africa they were taken from. The vast majority of these unfortunate individuals remain faceless, nameless, and silent to history. However, one of them did manage to survive capture, enslavement, and the voyage across the ocean. Olaudah Equiano was captured in what is now southern Nigeria in the 1750s and described his experiences in his best-selling narrative, *The Interesting Narrative of the Life of Olaudah Equiano, or Gustavus Vassa, the African:*

> *One day, when all our people were gone out to their works as usual, and only I and my dear sister were left to mind the house, two men and a woman got over our walls, and in a moment seized us both, and, without giving us time to cry out, or make resistance, they stopped our mouths, and ran off with us into the nearest*

wood. Here they tied our hands, and continued to carry us as far as they could, till night came on, when we reached a small house, where the robbers halted … We were then unbound, but were unable to take any food; and, being quite overpowered by fatigue and grief, our only relief was some sleep.[3]

During their march toward the coast, captured Africans were almost always shackled to discourage escape. A Scottish doctor and explorer named Mungo Park, who visited the western African coast in the 1790s, described the standard manner of binding captives:

They are commonly secured, by putting the right leg of one, and the left of another, into the same pair of fetters. By supporting the fetters with a string, they can walk, though very slowly. Every four slaves are likewise fastened together by the necks, with a strong rope of twisted thongs; and in the night an additional pair of fetters is put on their hands, and sometimes a light iron chain passed round their necks.[4]

The misery caused by these brutal and uncomfortable methods only contributed to the Africans' fear, especially once they realized they would be sold to white people. These fears were often stoked

Captured Africans bound for America endured terrible cruelty in Africa even before their life of slavery began, as shown in this painting.

THEY MADE HISTORY: OLAUDAH EQUIANO

Because few native Africans could read or write—let alone do so in English—few eyewitness accounts of the slave trade from a Black perspective have survived. The most substantial and famous of these accounts is by Olaudah Equiano. Born in 1745 in what is now Nigeria, he was kidnapped by Africans and taken to the Atlantic coast at about the age of 11. Equiano managed to survive the brutal journey across the ocean and ended up in Barbados. Not long afterward, he was sold to a planter in Virginia. One month later, a British naval officer purchased him and took him along on various military expeditions. This officer, Michael Henry Pascal, gave Olaudah the name Gustavus Vassa. During this period, Equiano learned English and became an accomplished sailor. In 1763, he was sold to a Quaker who allowed him to earn his freedom.

Once free, Equiano made England his home and became involved in the abolitionist movement, which sought to end slavery. At the urging of abolitionist friends, he wrote *The Interesting Narrative of the Life of Olaudah Equiano, or Gustavus Vassa, the African*, which described his capture and harrowing experiences in slavery. The book was published in 1789 and became a best seller. It was translated into Dutch, German, and Russian. Not only did it give a firsthand

by the belief that the Europeans would use them as a food source, which was an idea spread by some slave traders.

Whatever fears and expectations the captured people harbored during the forced march, they quickly learned that any resistance, or even accidental mistakes, would be met with severe punishment. Park described the harsh treatment of one enslaved person:

One of the Serawoolli slaves dropt [dropped] the load from his head, for which he was smartly whipped. The load was replaced;

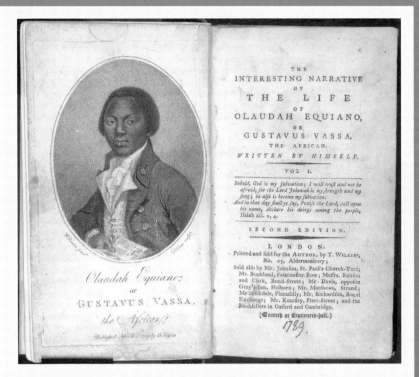

After receiving his freedom, Olaudah Equiano left the United States because he was afraid of being enslaved again.

account of the transatlantic slave trade, it also inspired the slave narrative genre, which became famous in America before the outbreak of the American Civil War. Olaudah Equiano died in London on March 31, 1797.

but he had not proceeded above a mile before he let it fall a second time, for which he received the same punishment. After this he travelled in great pain until about two o'clock, when we stopt [stopped] … The poor slave was now so completely exhausted … he lay motionless on the ground.[5]

Sold

After the harrowing march to the western coast of Africa, which came to be called Slave Coast, the captured Africans were kept in

FROM THE SOURCE:
THE INTERESTING NARRATIVE OF THE LIFE OF OLAUDAH EQUIANO

In his 1789 narrative, Olaudah Equiano described his months-long journey across West Africa after he and his sister were captured in their African village. Eventually, they reached the Atlantic coast:

All the nations and people I had hitherto [before this] passed through resembled our own in their manners, customs, and language: but I came at length to a country, the inhabitants of which differed from us in all those particulars ... [They] ate without washing their hands. They cooked also in iron pots, and had European cutlasses and [crossbows], which were unknown to us ... At last I came to the banks of a large river, which was covered with canoes, in which the people appeared to live with their household utensils ... I was put into one of these canoes, and we began to paddle and move along the river ... Thus I continued to travel, sometimes by land, sometimes by water, through different countries and various nations, till, at the end of six or seven months after I had been kidnapped, I arrived at the sea coast.[1]

1. Olaudah Equiano, *The Interesting Narrative of the Life of Olaudah Equiano, or Gustavus Vassa, the African. Written by Himself*, Vol. 1 (London, UK: G. Vassa, 1789), HTML e-book, docsouth.unc.edu/neh/equiano1/equiano1.html (accessed May 27, 2020).

cramped holding areas until they could be sold. These pens were often inside the basement of European coastal trading forts. The forts were equipped with cannons to deter rival European traders from attempting to steal people. Officials stayed in comfortable rooms on the upper floors of these structures, while the captives below were often packed into a space much too small, sometimes for months.

In this 19th-century illustration, a slave trader inspects an African sold into slavery.

At some point, the captives were presented to European slave traders, who would inspect them to decide if they would be able workers and could be sold for a good price. If they decided to buy a person, they paid the African ruler of a particular region or sometimes a leader's slave runner. Africans had no use for European money, so they received European goods, such as swords, knives, guns, ammunition, cotton cloth, tools, brass dishes, alcohol, and tobacco plants, as payment. White traders found the African slave traders to be sharp businessmen, hard to cheat and quick to bargain.

After the transaction, the captives were in the possession of the European traders and ready to be loaded onto ships for the New World. As grueling as the journey to the coast was and as difficult as the time waiting in a fort dungeon must have been, the journey to the Americas could be even more dangerous.

How You See History

1. Do you think the African practice of slavery helped Europeans feel justified in their own slavery practices? Why or why not?

2. What might have happened if more Europeans could have traveled farther into Africa?

3. Why is it important to read narratives of people who were enslaved?

STOWAGE OF THE BRITISH SLAVE SHIP "BROOKES" UNDER THE
REGULATED SLAVE TRADE
Act of 1788.

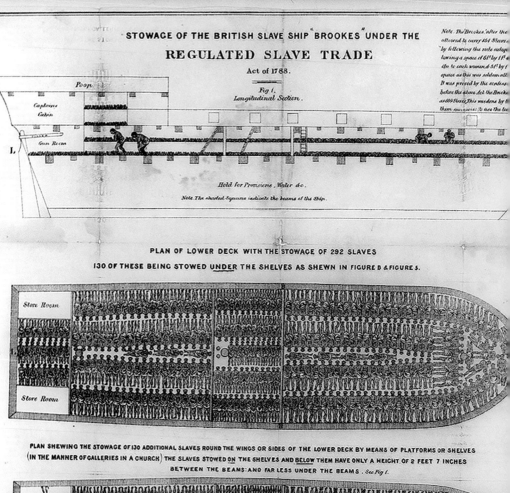

Fig 1.
Longitudinal Section.

Note. The Brookes, after the
allowed to carry 454 Slaves
by following the rule adopted
leaving a space of 6ft by 1ft
also to each woman 5ft by 1
spaces as this was seldom all
It was proved by the confess
before the above Act the Brooke
as 609 Slaves. This reckons by th
them in as 1 to two tho' lea

Hold for Provisions, Water &c.

Note. The shaded Squares indicate the beams of the Ship.

PLAN OF LOWER DECK WITH THE STOWAGE OF 292 SLAVES
130 OF THESE BEING STOWED UNDER THE SHELVES AS SHEWN IN FIGURE D & FIGURE S.

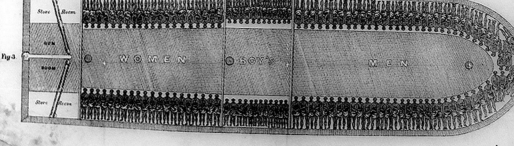

PLAN SHEWING THE STOWAGE OF 130 ADDITIONAL SLAVES ROUND THE WINGS OR SIDES OF THE LOWER DECK BY MEANS OF PLATFORMS OR SHELVES
(IN THE MANNER OF GALLERIES IN A CHURCH) THE SLAVES STOWED ON THE SHELVES AND BELOW THEM HAVE ONLY A HEIGHT OF 2 FEET 7 INCHES
BETWEEN THE BEAMS: AND FAR LESS UNDER THE BEAMS. See Fig 1.

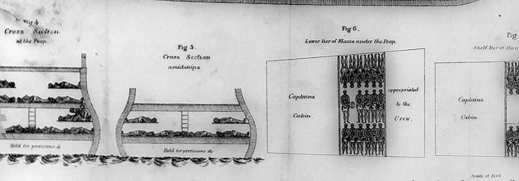

CHAPTER FOUR

THE MIDDLE PASSAGE

When the Europeans had bought enough captives in Africa to fill their ships—often between 150 and 600 Africans—they prepared them for the trip to the Americas, the so-called Middle Passage. It was called the Middle Passage because it was the middle voyage for the ships that had traveled from Europe and, after stopping in the Americas, would travel back to Europe. It was the second grueling journey for those who had been forcibly marched from the interior of Africa to coastal trading forts. This journey to come was terrifying because their countrymen who had made it before them never came back to tell the tale.

These Africans would be treated as living cargo, respected little more than cattle: inspected, branded with a hot iron, and loaded below the deck of a ship into an extremely uncomfortable and cramped area that would become riddled with disease. Coupled with the cruel treatment of the crew—denying the enslaved Africans enough food and drink to maintain their health—many found the situation so impossible that they sought to end it in any way that they could. For some, this meant suicide; for others, mutiny.

Preparations

Because profits and margins were the most important parts of a European slave trader's life, they needed to ensure that as many enslaved

This image shows how tightly captives could be packed on a ship. A 1788 British act required more space for each enslaved person.

Africans as possible completed the voyage overseas in good physical shape. Accordingly, they carefully inspected each captive who arrived on the coast. Those who seemed sickly or weak—and therefore unlikely to survive the Middle Passage—were rejected. A Dutch trader named Willem Bosman, who witnessed the inspection and loading of captives onto ships for the Middle Passage around 1700, wrote:

> They [the captives] are all brought out together in a large plain; where, by our surgeons, they are thoroughly examined, and that naked, both too men and women, without the least distinction or modesty. Those which are approved as good, are set on one side; in the mean while a burning iron, with the arms [symbol] or name of the [trading] company, lies in the fire, with which ours [our captives] are marked.[1]

While the guards and sailors loaded the inspected and branded Africans onto the ship, they also loaded the supplies of food and water that would be needed during the long voyage. Whenever possible, the ship captains obtained a native or local food that the captives were accustomed to eating. By doing this, there was less chance that the Africans would get sick and die during the voyage. If too many Africans died during the passage, the owners of the ship or the sponsors of the expedition would lose profits. In many parts of West Africa, the most common local food was yams. The French captain Jean Barbot estimated that a store of around 100,000 yams was necessary to sustain a shipload of 500 Africans during the Middle Passage. Slave traders negotiated deals to buy large supplies of yams from local chieftains before they took a shipment of Africans. The sellers ran hard bargains for the yams, just as they did for the enslaved people themselves. The slave traders also bought wood, fresh water, and goats and hogs (to supply milk and meat for the ship's crew) from the locals before they left port with their human cargo.

Terrifying Trip
With the captives and the necessary food and water loaded, the slave ships embarked on the journey across the Atlantic. Few eyewitness accounts of this terrible journey written by Africans who actually suffered through the ordeal have survived. This is not surprising, since

FROM THE SOURCE:
A NEW AND ACCURATE DESCRIPTION OF THE COAST OF GUINEA

Willem Bosman was a Dutch captain and slave trader who wrote a book called *A New and Accurate Description of the Coast of Guinea* around 1705. He provided his biased view of the Middle Passage of the slave trade:

> You would really wonder to see how these slaves live on board; for though their number sometimes amounts to six or seven hundred, yet by the careful management of our masters of ships, they are so [well] regulated, that it seems incredible. And in this particular our nation exceeds all other Europeans; for as the French, Portuguese, and English slave-ships are always foul and stinking; on the contrary, ours are for the most part clean and neat.
>
> The slaves are fed three times a day with indifferent good victuals [foods], and much better than they eat in their own country. Their lodging place is divided into two parts; one of which is appointed for the men, the other for the women, each sex being kept apart. Here they lie as close together as it is possible for them to be crowded.[1]

1. Quoted in "An Eyewitness Describes the Slave Trade in Guinea," Cengage Learning, college.cengage.com/history/primary/eyewitness.htm (accessed May 16, 2020).

many of them died on the voyage, and many more went on to live the rest of their lives in the Americas or other exploitation colonies.

Among the handful of enslaved Africans who wrote about the experience was Olaudah Equiano. His description of the Middle Passage is revealing. Particularly memorable, he wrote, was the foul smell in the ship's hold, where hundreds of prisoners lay or sat shackled, sweating, vomiting, and in some cases, bleeding from various skin sores:

I was soon put down under the decks, and there I received such a salutation [greeting] in my nostrils as I had never experienced in my life: so that, with the loathsomeness of the stench, and [people] crying together, I became so sick and low that I was not able to cat [eat], nor had I the least desire to taste any thing ... To my grief, two of the white men offered me eatables [food]; and, on my refusing to eat, one of them held me fast by the hands ... and tied my feet, while the other flogged [whipped] me severely. I had never experienced any thing of this kind before.[2]

The packed, unbearably stinking conditions below the decks were also described by Alexander Falconbridge, a British ship doctor. He wrote:

The height, sometimes, between decks, was only eighteen inches; so that the unfortunate human beings could not turn around, or even on their sides, the elevation being less than the breadth of their shoulders; and here they are usually chained to the decks by the neck and legs. In such a place the sense of misery and suffocation is so great, that the Negroes ... are driven to frenzy.[3]

During the voyage, small groups would be allowed to spend some time on deck in the open air. These moments of comfort were brief, however. Soon, the prisoners were forced to return to the nightmarish conditions below, as Equiano recalled:

This 19th-century drawing shows how Africans sometimes traveled with nothing to keep them warm or to provide them any comfort at all on the long voyage across the Atlantic.

The closeness of the place, and the heat of the climate, added to the number [of prisoners] in the ship, which was so crowded that each had scarcely room to turn himself, almost suffocated us. This produced copious [a lot of] perspirations, so that the air soon became unfit for respiration, from a variety of loathsome smells, and brought on a sickness among the slaves, of which many died … In this situation I expected every hour to share the fate of my companions, some of whom were almost daily brought upon deck at the point of death, which I began to hope would soon put an end to my miseries.[4]

Resistance

Olaudah Equiano was not alone in thinking that perhaps death was better than the brutal realities of the Middle Passage. In fact, a few of the enslaved Africans who shared the ship with Equiano went so far as to attempt suicide. He wrote, "One day, when we had a smooth sea and moderate wind, two of my wearied countrymen who were chained together … preferring death to such a life of misery … jumped into the sea." Seeing this, another prisoner who was on deck also hurled himself overboard. "I believe many more would very soon have done the same," Equiano wrote, "if they had not been prevented by the ship's crew, who were instantly alarmed." Two of the three who had jumped overboard drowned, while the third was rescued and then savagely beaten "for thus attempting to prefer death to slavery."[5] Equiano's experiences were not at all unusual or uncommon. Similar scenes of suicide, hopelessness, and brutality could have been viewed on any number of ships during the Middle Passage.

Many of the enslaved Africans were so traumatized and exhausted by their ordeal that they lacked the energy and boldness to resist their captors in any meaningful way. However, surviving evidence shows that some of them did resist. Violent outbursts occurred on many slave ships. Sometimes, these escalated into full-scale rebellions or mutinies—a few of which were successful, or almost so. Slave ship captain Willem Bosman described one nearly successful insurrection aboard a Dutch vessel:

Unknown to any of the ship's crew, [the captives] possessed themselves of a hammer, with which, in a short time, they broke all

their fetters in pieces ... After this, they came above deck, and fell upon our men, some of whom they grievously wounded and would certainly have mastered [taken] the ship if a French and English ship had not very fortunately happened to lie by us; who perceiving by our firing a distressed-gun, that something was in disorder on board, immediately came to our assistance ... about twenty of them [the captives] were killed.[6]

This illustration from a 1904 book depicts Africans throwing themselves overboard to escape their captivity.

Though documentation of slave rebellions during the Middle Passage are few, there were likely hundreds of such attempts at freedom by the African captives. Unfortunately for the captives, most ended up in failure and death. While there are some accounts of captives jumping overboard and swimming back to safety, the results of uprisings were overwhelmingly negative. Despite the opposition of their African prisoners, the Europeans did not stop or slow down their operations. Instead, to attempt to avoid such incidents, experienced ship captains took a number of precautions, including frequent checking that leg irons and other restraints were secure and pointing cannons at the door of the hold.

After an unsuccessful rebellion, captains and crewmembers served severe punishments to the leaders and participants. Beatings with whips or ropes were common, as were other kinds of painful torture. Some rebellion leaders were shot, thrown overboard, or cut into pieces. There are disturbing accounts of captains dealing with uprisings by causing immense pain to the Africans who attempted them and making the other captives watch.

HISTORY HAPPENED HERE: THE AMISTAD MEMORIAL

Perhaps the most famous slave rebellion on a ship took place on the *Amistad* in 1839. An African onboard named Sengbe Pieh (or Joseph Cinqué) used a nail to free himself from his chains. He led 53 captives to take over the schooner. The Africans found knives, killed the captain and other crew, and tried to force the two Spanish men who had bought them (illegally) to sail them back to Africa from Cuba. The men tricked the Africans and sailed to the United States instead, hoping to be rescued. The U.S. Navy took the ship to Connecticut, where the Africans were put on trial for murder and piracy. Eventually, the case went to the U.S. Supreme Court, which decided that since the Africans had been transported from Africa illegally, they should be freed. The survivors sailed back to Africa, to today's Sierra Leone, on the *Amistad* in 1842.

Today, a bronze memorial stands outside New Haven City Hall and County Courthouse in Connecticut, where the Africans on the *Amistad* were jailed while awaiting trial.

Death of Capt. Ferrer, the Captain of the Amistad, July, 1839.

The revolt on the *Amistad* began after the ship's cook told the captives that they were to be killed and then cooked. The terrified Africans later killed the cook and the *Amistad*'s captain, as shown here.

Deadly Consequences

Rebellions undoubtedly contributed to the high death toll on ships undergoing the Middle Passage. Though only about 55 accounts of

THEY MADE HISTORY: SENGBE PIEH

As the leader of the *Amistad* rebellion, Sengbe Pieh became a symbol of slave resistance. He was born around 1811 in West Africa. When he was in his 20s, four Black men kidnapped him. His family did not know where he went. He was forced to march for days to the coast, where he was made to board a Portuguese slave ship with hundreds of others. Sengbe Pieh saw many people die as they traveled west to Cuba. Since it was illegal to take enslaved people to Cuba at that time (though slavery itself was legal), Sengbe Pieh and his fellow captives were snuck onto land at night and passed off as Cuban-born. It was in Cuba that he was given the name Joseph Cinqué, sold, and loaded onto the *Amistad*.

The enslaved Africans on the *Amistad* were supposed to be sold to Cuban plantation owners. However, after the ship's cook told the Africans that they would be killed and eaten, Sengbe Pieh began to plan an escape. He freed himself and the other captives and overtook the crew. When American sailors caught the ship near the shore of the United States, Sengbe Pieh and the others were jailed. During one of the trials, Sengbe Pieh spoke on behalf of the Africans, explaining the ordeal they had been through. After he was freed, Sengbe Pieh returned to Africa. Little is known about the rest of his life.

mutinies were recorded between 1699 and 1845, a modern estimate suggests that one out of every ten slave voyages experienced at least an attempt at mutiny, which would have resulted in deaths. People opting to die by suicide would have added to the high numbers of dead. Likely thousands killed themselves by jumping overboard, refusing to eat, or other such methods. (Some captains punished attempted suicide by cutting off a slave's limb; this punishment could eventually lead to death too.)

However, conditions onboard the ships were the cause of most of the deaths. The lack of space in the slave hold was a dangerous issue.

If an onboard rebellion did not succeed, enslaved Africans were treated even more brutally by the crew.

On some vessels, enslaved Africans were packed so tightly below the deck that many of them had no option but to lie on top of others. Those who were beneath sometimes suffocated.

With hundreds of people on each ship, the need for fresh water was always serious. Many slave ships lacked the room to carry enough water. Plus, the Africans in the hold would have required even more because of the extreme heat below the deck. It is estimated that captives received one-quarter or less of the amount they needed. When water was low, it was saved for the crew, so captives might have gone days without it. The resulting severe dehydration caused many health problems, if not deaths.

Disease was another major problem during the transatlantic slave voyages. Illnesses such as dysentery, measles, and smallpox easily circulated throughout a vessel, and the unsanitary environment encouraged bacteria and viruses to spread. They hit the Africans especially hard because their immune systems were weakened by severe malnutrition and because of their confined space. Enslaved Africans were introduced to new diseases carried by the European crew, while the crew contracted the disease called yellow fever in Africa. Both captives and crew sometimes developed ophthalmia, an eye disease that can dim vision and cause temporary or total blindness.

PAST MEETS PRESENT: THE SLAVE WRECKS PROJECT

In addition to inhumane treatment and poor conditions onboard the slave ships, the Middle Passage also subjected African captives to the dangers of ocean storms, which sometimes damaged or even wrecked the ships, sending many to watery graves.

In 1794, a ship called the *São José* was wrecked off the southern coast of Africa on its way to Brazil from East Africa. The vessel had struck a rock and began to sink. While the crew and some Africans made it to shore, more than half of the 400 prisoners onboard drowned. The ship was lost for hundreds of years.

In 2013, a group called the Slave Wrecks Project, or SWP, identified the remains of a wrecked vessel as the *São José*. Using modern technology, they studied fragile artifacts still within the sunken ship, including shackles that would have been used to bind captives. This is the first wreck of a slave ship ever found. SWP, a collaboration between organizations such as the Smithsonian, George Washington University, and other groups, continues to work to find other shipwrecks in order to shine a light on the memory of the transatlantic slave trade.

Even ships with doctors aboard could not stop the spread of disease. Doctors knew little about germs back then. Also, they could do nothing about the lack of space in the slave hold. The one sickness doctors did treat was scurvy, which they fought by administering vitamin C through foods. However, they were helpless against many other life-threatening illnesses.

Many of the issues during the Atlantic crossings could have been avoided. However, a lack of empathy, respect, and care for the human lives below the deck kept the death toll high. An infamous case of cruelty occurred on the *Zong*, a British slave ship that made the Atlantic crossing in 1781. After many days at sea, the vessel was short of water, and numerous enslaved people onboard were sick. Many Africans

Even after slavery was outlawed in many places, illegal slave trading continued. In this image, slave traders throw people overboard to avoid being prosecuted.

had already died in the poor conditions, and crew members began to suffer as well. The captain, Luke Collingwood, made the decision to throw more than 130 captives into the ocean to stop the spread of disease. He later tried to collect insurance on his "lost cargo."

The enslaved Africans had to bear their terrible conditions onboard ships for about seven weeks. Many did not survive. Captives were thrown overboard as they died. One trader noted that sharks followed ships that threw bodies into the water. Historians estimate that 10 to 20 percent of captives were lost during the Middle Passage, which is between 1 million and 2 million people. The survivors of the voyage did not have anything to celebrate, however. They may have lived through the voyage, but their destination held little comfort for them. They were about to begin their difficult, dangerous life of enslavement.

How You See History

1. Why do you think enslaved Africans were bought in good health but then subjected to such poor treatment on ships?

2. Why did many Middle Passage captains refuse to transport fewer people on their ships, reducing the problems on board?

3. What other factors might contribute to our lack of knowledge about the number of Africans who died during the Middle Passage of the transatlantic slave trade?

CHAPTER FIVE

INTO A LIFE OF SLAVERY

Finally reaching the Americas after weeks at sea must have held some relief for enslaved Africans who were suffocating in the small holds of slave ships. However, even fresh air and the ability to move again were little consolation when faced with a lifetime of slavery ahead.

At whatever port the slave ship reached, the journey for the enslaved was not necessarily over. Some were marched many miles over land to plantations, mines, houses, or other work sites. Others had to take additional water routes to their destination. Over the course of the entire transatlantic slave trade, about 45 percent of all captive Africans who survived the voyages were taken to Brazil, a colony of Portugal. About 37 percent were transported to Caribbean islands held by the British, French, Dutch, and Danish. A little over 10 percent of all enslaved Africans were taken to parts of South America controlled by Spain. And more than 3 percent of African captives, or about 388,000 people, were sent to North America.

No matter where in the New World the enslaved Africans found themselves, they were in unknown territory. They saw new kinds of plants and animals, witnessed strange customs, and were spoken to in languages they did not understand. Most must have been terrified

Enslaved people are guarded as they mine for diamonds in Brazil in this 19th-century print.

to reach this new land and then be sold, likely separating them from others they had met on the voyage. No matter how kind their owner might have seemed, most could never hope for freedom again. Some found themselves up against the harshest of owners, with a punishment behind every perceived slight. Most did what they could to just survive. Some found their lives in the New World unbearable.

In a Strange Land

Typically, the newly arrived Africans quickly learned to follow the rules set down by owners. After their long, painful voyage across the ocean, most captives were exhausted and fearful, and therefore quiet. They largely did as they were directed, allowing others to clean them up, lead them off the ship, and put them into holding pens.

There were exceptions to this trend, however. One, which has become legendary, occurred in 1803 on one of the islands off the coast of Georgia. A slave ship carrying a group of Igbos, people native to present-day Nigeria, pulled into port on the small island of St. Simons after its trip across the Atlantic. The guards began to lead the prisoners down the gangplanks and onto the beach. The expectation was that the enslaved Africans would obediently do what they were told and their captors would have little trouble preparing them for the upcoming auction, where they were to be sold to plantation owners.

What the guards did not know was that the members of this particular group of Igbos had a long, proud tradition of refusing to live in servitude. Onlookers were surprised, therefore, when the first few captives who stepped onto the island did not follow the guards. Instead, the Africans walked, silently and purposefully, toward nearby Dunbar Creek and drowned themselves. Ignoring the shouts, warnings, and whips of the guards, every enslaved Igbo who left the ship followed those first few leaders in an orderly manner, down the banks and into the water. The line of Igbos went deeper and deeper into the water. Despite the efforts of the guards to rescue the Africans, many Igbos drowned.

The mass suicide of the Igbos and their display of powerful cultural traditions in the face of permanent enslavement were unusual. The vast majority of Africans who arrived in the Americas were likely relieved that they had made it across the ocean alive. They wanted to

FROM THE SOURCE:
A PLANTER'S PERSPECTIVE

As enslaved people arrived in the Americas, their enslavers sometimes justified their exploitation of the captives by suggesting that the Africans were not really against living in servitude. A Jamaican planter named Bryan Edwards claimed that most slaves were not badly treated and actually looked forward to being sold:

> Although there is something extremely shocking to a humane and cultivated mind, in the idea of beholding a numerous body of our unfortunate fellow-creatures, in captivity and exile ... and sold like a herd of cattle, yet I could never perceive ... that the Negroes themselves were oppressed with many of those painful sensations which a person unaccustomed to the scene would naturally attribute to such apparent wretchedness ... [They] commonly express great eagerness to be sold; presenting themselves ... with cheerfulness and alacrity [eagerness] for selection.[1]

Observations such as this circulated the false idea that enslaved Africans were willing participants in the practice of slavery, helping owners and traders defend their actions.

1. Bryan Edwards, *The History, Civil and Commercial, of the British West Indies*, vol. 2 (London, UK: T. Miller, 1819), pp. 151–153.

stay alive as long as they could—which meant obedience. Many probably thought that, given time and fortunate circumstances, they might find a way to regain their freedom. In the meantime, they faced the reality of new, strange surroundings. The society of their white enslavers was quite different from their own, and they needed to learn what they could about white culture to ensure their continued survival.

This was the attitude that Olaudah Equiano adopted upon his arrival in Barbados, in the Lesser Antilles island chain, in the 1750s. He was immediately struck by how different the houses looked compared

TO BE SOLD on board the Ship *Bance-Island*, on tuesday the 6th of *May* next, at *Afhley-Ferry*; a choice cargo of about 250 fine healthy NEGROES, juft arrived from the Windward & Rice Coaft. —The utmoft care has already been taken, and fhall be continued, to keep them free from the leaft danger of being infected with the SMALL-POX, no boat having been on board, and all other communication with people from *Charles-Town* prevented.

Auftin, Laurens, & Appleby.

N. B. Full one Half of the above Negroes have had the SMALL-POX in their own Country.

This newspaper from around 1700 in Boston, Massachusetts, advertises Africans to be sold onboard the ship they arrived in.

to those in his native land. He was also amazed at the sight of people on horseback. Although horses existed in Africa, he personally had never seen one. He wrote:

> We were conducted immediately to the merchant's yard, where we were all pent up together like so many sheep in a fold, without regard to sex or age. As every object was new to me every thing I saw filled me with surprise … But I was still more astonished on seeing people on horseback. I did not know what this could mean; and indeed I thought these people were full of nothing but magical arts.[1]

Most enslaved Africans did not have long to sit around and think about their strange surroundings once their ships reached American harbors. The majority, especially those in reasonably good physical condition, were sold as quickly as possible to local planters and white people of other professions. Often, Black families and couples were separated and sold to different people at the end of the Middle Passage. Some implored to be bought together. Sometimes their pleading helped, but sometimes it was useless.

Sold Again

One of the most common methods of sale, especially in the early years of the slave trade, was the scramble. In this format, potential buyers purchased a number of tickets before seeing any enslaved person. Then, with the group of buyers assembled, the gates of the Africans' holding area were opened, and the buyers rushed in, grabbed as many Africans as they had tickets, and took them to a cashier. There, they would hand in their pre-purchased tickets and walk away with their chosen Africans. A rare eyewitness description of such a scramble sale survived in Equiano's narrative:

> On a signal given, (as the beat of a drum) the buyers rush at once into the yard where the slaves are confined, and make choice of that parcel they like best. The noise and clamour with which this is attended, and the eagerness visible in the countenances [faces] of the buyers, serve ... to increase the apprehensions [fears] of the terrified Africans ... In this manner, without scruple [hesitation], are relations and friends separated, most of them never to see each other again.[2]

Perhaps because it was so rushed and hectic, the scramble method became less common over time and was replaced by the more orderly slave auction. A description of such an auction was written by George Pinckard, a British doctor who traveled on a number of slave ships. He recalled:

> A long table was placed in the middle of a large room. At one end was seated the auctioneer: at the other was placed a chair for the

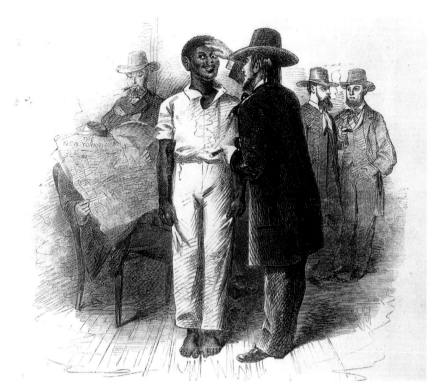

In this illustration from around 1850, a prospective buyer carefully examines an African.

negroes to stand upon, in order to be exposed to the view of the purchasers … All being in readiness, the slaves were brought in, one at a time, and placed upon the chair before the bidders, who handled and inspected them, with as little concern as if they had been examining cattle in Smithfield market. They turned them about, felt them, viewed their shape and their limbs, looked into their mouths, made them jump and throw out their arms, and subjected them to all the means of trial as if dealing for a horse, or any other brute animal.[3]

Regardless of the manner in which the Africans were sold off, they ultimately had the same fate. They were enslaved by someone who would control them for the rest of their lives in most cases. However, a minority of captive Africans who crossed the Atlantic to the Americas endured two, three, or more sales. Passed from one owner to another, they sometimes ended up crossing the ocean again, as it was not uncommon for American enslavers to sell off a few of their enslaved people to European buyers.

Equiano, who witnessed these trades firsthand, described them in his work. Unlike most Africans who landed in the Americas, he was sold several times and traveled to foreign lands. In the Barbados scramble described in his narrative, a planter from Virginia purchased him and transported him to a plantation in that faraway British colony. Equiano had barely begun to work on the plantation when an Englishman arrived. Equiano later wrote:

> One day the captain of a merchant ship, called the Industrious Bee, came on some business to my master's house. This gentleman, whose name was Michael Henry Pascal … liked me so well that he made a purchase of me. I think I have often heard him say he gave thirty or forty pounds sterling for me … I was carried on board a fine large ship, loaded with tobacco … and just ready to sail for England.[4]

Pascal and two other men who later owned Equiano treated him with some kindness and actually provided him with an education. He was eventually permitted to buy his freedom. However, the vast majority of enslaved people did not have opportunities like this. Millions

In this drawing from around 1830, a mother and child cling to each other while being auctioned. Families were often separated in the New World.

HISTORY HAPPENED HERE: BUTLER ISLAND PLANTATION

Butler Island Plantation near Darien, Georgia, was one of the largest plantations in the South. It is managed today by the Georgia Department of Natural Resources and open to the public.

Built in the 1790s, the plantation is located on an island that was ideal for growing rice. Pierce Butler owned the land and several hundred enslaved people in the 1830s. His wife, a former actress named Fanny Kemble, was an abolitionist who tried to persuade her husband to improve the lives of the enslaved Africans. Eventually, he would not let her speak about it. She wrote about her short stay at the plantation and the harsh conditions there, calling the published work *Journal of a Residence on a Georgian Plantation*. The couple later divorced.

In 1857, to pay off Butler's large debts, 436 of his enslaved workers were auctioned off in Savannah, Georgia. This sale was called "the Weeping Time" by some because so many enslaved people were wrenched from the only homes and friends they had ever known. It was the largest slave auction in U.S. history.

Newspaper writer Mortimer Thomson wrote about the event. He reported that some of the enslaved Africans acted cheerfully to please potential buyers who seemed kind, even as they were "pulling their mouths open to see their teeth,

were repeatedly beaten, never given an education, and never had the slightest chance of gaining their freedom. Instead, they became part of a large-scale institution in which a few white people controlled practically every aspect of the lives of large numbers of enslaved people.

To Punish and Control

The relationship between slave owners and the enslaved was packed with tension. Enslavers were always trying to get the most work

In this photograph of the Butler Island Plantation property, you can see the remains of a rice mill and the plantation house in the background.

> pinching their limbs to find how muscular they were, walking them up and down to detect any signs of lameness, making them stoop and bend in different ways that they might be certain there was no concealed rupture or wound." However, the artificial cheerfulness did not mask "an expression of heavy grief"[1] in all, he noted.

1. Quoted in "The Weeping Time," Africans in America, PBS.org, www.pbs.org/wgbh/aia/part4/4p2918.html (accessed May 18, 2020).

out of their "property," but pushing them too hard could result in rebellion. Maintaining control was a constant worry, especially for those who owned a large number of people. Sometimes, the threat of violence was enough to keep enslaved laborers obedient. Other times, one unlucky worker would be singled out and beaten in front of the others as a warning to all who were not subservient. The constant fear of punishment was an effective deterrent to those who had no power.

PAST MEETS PRESENT: A MODERN SLAVE AUCTION

Just as slavery still exists in different forms today, the slave auction is not entirely extinct. In November 2017, a video surfaced of men being sold at an auction in the African country of Libya. One auctioneer could be heard describing a man as a "big strong digger."[1] This was the first definitive proof that such a slave trade exists. Some of the captives were even branded like those of years ago.

It is believed that migrants and refugees who were on their way to Europe were swept up in a slavery ring in Libya. Many such people are trying to escape war, poverty, lack of employment, and the effects of climate change in their own countries. They have little money or power and are vulnerable to slave traffickers, who are often armed with weapons. Many groups around the world demanded that the Libyan government find such slave auctions and end them. This effort is still ongoing.

1. Quoted in Jennifer Bihm and Kimberlee Buck, "Libya Slave Trade, a Heinous Modern Day Slave Auction," *Los Angeles Sentinel*, December 14, 2017, lasentinel. net/libya-slave-trade-a-heinous-modern-day-slave-auction.html.

The desire to be free and hatred of their life of servitude was never far from the minds of most enslaved people, though. Some challenged their fate in small ways, such as working slowly, pretending to be ill, or stealing small things from their owners. If caught, the punishments ranged from slight to cruel, depending on the enslaver and the transgression.

The worst penalties were reserved for those who tried to run away. Running away was a difficult and dangerous risk. Enslaved people usually had no individuals they could go to for help. On the run, they were vulnerable to dying of starvation or exposure in bad weather. Slave catchers were always on the lookout for runaways. Those who could not bear a life of slavery took the ultimate gamble, sometimes having no choice but to leave loved ones behind. If that gamble failed,

THEY MADE HISTORY: GEORGE WASHINGTON

In the United States, few people are more famous than George Washington. The American Revolution general and first U.S. president is perhaps the most well-known Founding Father. George Washington also owned enslaved people.

Born on February 22, 1732, in Virginia, George Washington was the son of a prosperous landowner. He learned to become a surveyor but then pursued a life in the military. During the French and Indian War (1754–1763), his military exploits helped him rise in the ranks to brigadier general. He then entered politics, serving in the Virginia House of Burgesses. Washington became part of the movement to make the British colonies in America independent of Great Britain, eventually becoming the commander-in-chief of the Continental Army and later serving as president of the United States. After the war and when his presidential duties permitted it, Washington was at the plantation he inherited, Mount Vernon, overseeing his lands and enslaved people.

Some of his surviving correspondence discusses slave discipline. At least 47 enslaved people tried to run away from Mount Vernon and other properties owned by Washington. Washington approved of punishments, including whippings, for such behavior. When people continued to run away, he sold them. At the end of his life, Washington made the decision to free all the enslaved people on his farms after his wife, Martha, passed away. Washington died in 1799.

they found themselves at the mercy of their enslavers, who sometimes showed no mercy. Some enslavers used physical restraints on runaways or otherwise disobedient people. These could include collars of leather or metal, sometimes attached to ropes or chains much like an animal would wear.

Olaudah Equiano remembered seeing enslavers hang chains or even hooks around the necks of enslaved people, making the wearer's

An exhausted enslaved African is whipped by an overseer in this illustration from 1826.

neck hang under the weight and removing the possibility of another escape. He also wrote about other torturous devices used to punish and control an enslaved woman who worked in a house:

> The poor creature was cruelly loaded with various kinds of iron machines; she had one particularly on her head, which locked her mouth so fast that she could scarcely speak; and could not eat nor drink. I was much astonished and shocked at this contrivance, which I learned afterwards was called the iron muzzle.[5]

Other known punishments included branding skin with hot irons, slicing noses, cutting off toes or fingers, pulling out teeth, and scalding with boiling water. Enslaved women were sometimes sexually assaulted by their owners or overseers. Seldom did any of these actions result in negative consequences for the aggressor.

In fact, the law was usually on the side of the enslaver. One North Carolina law, similar to many others at the time, gave slave owners almost unrestricted power in dealing with runaways:

This man is demonstrating a device that enslaved people who ran away had to wear. A bell was hung on top to make noise.

In all such cases [of a runaway] … the sheriff of the said county [may] take such power with him as he shall think fit and necessary for going in search and pursuit … If any slave or slaves, against whom proclamation hath [accusation has] been thus issued, stay out, and do not immediately return home, it shall be lawful for any person or persons whatsoever to kill and destroy such slave or slaves by such ways and means as he shall think fit, without accusation or impeachment of any crime.[6]

Such an inhumane system as slavery could not last. The cruelty of the institution drew more and more people to the cause of abolition, or the end of slavery. Countries in Europe and then the Americas began to outlaw importing enslaved Africans and then abolish slavery altogether. Sadly, many generations of enslaved people had to endure hard, often unnaturally short lives of captivity before slavery came to an end.

How You See History

1. Why did most enslaved people offer little resistance upon landing in the New World?

2. How did slave sales and auctions contribute to the dehumanization of enslaved people?

3. Why do you think many enslaved people risked punishment with small acts of resistance, such as doing their work slowly?

CHAPTER SIX

THE ABOLITION MOVEMENT

Many European nations had an intense desire to increase their power by establishing and investing in their colonies in the Americas. That power became synonymous with the success of colonial plantations' cash crops. The demand for cheap plantation labor outweighed reservations about the morality of the transatlantic slave trade. Many people, including slave traders, merchants, and owners of large farms, became wealthy through the exploitation of enslaved Africans. In order to keep up their profits, they relied on slave labor. Government officials, too, had a stake in slavery. Slavery meant a strong economy, which reflected well on their leadership. Thus, global ambitions became tied to the Middle Passage, and calls to abolish slavery were few and faint until the 18th century.

Another hindrance to early efforts of abolitionists was the support of slavery by many Christian religious leaders, who formulated ways of justifying the practice. They sometimes used the Bible to validate owning people, since heroes of the Old Testament had done so. They also pointed out that Jesus Christ did not explicitly condemn slavery in the New Testament. Additionally, some Christians alleged that slavery was actually helping Africans by placing them in "civilized" places and exposing them to Christian beliefs. Even without this

◀ The abolition, or abolitionist, movement was created to stop the practice of slavery and free enslaved people such as those depicted here.

justification, years of dehumanizing enslaved people and labeling them as property—literally branding them like cattle—had skewed perspectives about the slave trade. Many who might have supported an abolition movement earlier were swayed not to because of European culture of the time.

Still, beginning in the mid- to late 1700s, the abolitionist movement began to spread in Europe and the Americas. Inspired by philosophers of the Enlightenment movement and propelled by religious groups such as the Quakers, millions of people began to believe that all humans had rights, including the right to liberty and equality, and that slavery was immoral and un-Christian. This was the foundation upon which the abolition movement built itself for more than 100 years before the ending of the transatlantic slave trade and finally the institution of slavery itself.

Shedding Light on Slavery

The great intellectual turning point that formed the basis of the abolitionist movement was the emergence and spread of the European Enlightenment and the new ideas advocated by those who were considered its leaders. The Enlightenment was a movement of thinkers, writers, and artists who lived in the 17th and 18th centuries. Most of these individuals were British or French, but they influenced intellectuals in nations and colonies throughout Europe and the Americas. Enlightenment thinkers strongly supported religious freedom, the use of reason and science, fair government, and basic human rights, including freedom of speech and expression.

One of the primary goals of Enlightenment thinkers was to create a spirit of political and social reform. That was part of the inspiration for the title of the movement: The activists believed they were "enlightened" from a past of inequality and social injustice. As such, many believed, their duty was to spread their new understanding across the world. Some of the biggest targets for these thinkers were despots (absolute rulers such as emperors, who did not have to follow laws), religious zealots (those who persecuted others who did not share their beliefs), and slave merchants and owners.

However, it quickly became clear to abolitionists that outlawing slavery itself was going to be a long, difficult process. The institution of slavery was a crucial part of politics, the economy, and daily life for millions of white people. Accordingly, no contemporary government, even the most enlightened, seemed to be ready for what was then seen as a very drastic move. The fact that the founders of the United States, who advocated freedom and equality, did not immediately end slavery clearly illustrates this attitude. As a result, abolitionists instead adopted the strategy of accomplishing a more realistic goal first: abolishing the slave trade. Once that goal had been achieved, they reasoned, there would be a better chance of eliminating slavery itself.

Getting the Word Out

The abolitionists devoted their powerful influence toward denouncing the trafficking of human beings. This resulted in an increasing flood of books, essays, newspaper articles, and public speeches by famous figures. Abolitionists steadily won over ministers and other clergymen, who lectured to their followers about the evils of the trade. In this way, people who had once taken slavery for granted were converted to the abolitionist cause.

A famous case of such conversion was that of John Newton, a British ship captain who worked on slave ships but later joined the abolitionist movement. His change of heart and subsequent opposition to the slave trade were fuel for the abolitionists' strong commitment to ending the slave trade. In one of his many surviving writings dedicated to fighting the slave trade, Newton declared:

> I hope it always will be a subject of humiliating reflection to me, that I was, once, an active instrument, in a business at which my heart now shudders ... Perhaps what I have said of myself may be applicable to the nation at large. The Slave Trade was always unjustifiable; but inattention and interest prevented, for a time, the evil from being perceived. It is otherwise at present; the mischiefs and evils, connected with it, have been, of late years, represented with such undeniable evidence, and are now, so generally known, that I suppose there is hardly an objection can be made, to the wish of thousands, perhaps of millions, for the suppression of this Trade, but upon the ground of political expedience.[1]

Newton was widely admired for his aggressive stance against slavery. He was passionate in his condemnation of the slave trade in the following remarks:

> If the trade is at present carried on to the same extent, and nearly in the same manner, while we are delaying from year to year to put a stop to our part in it, the blood of many thousands of our helpless, much injured fellow creatures, is crying against us. The pitiable state of the survivors, who are torn from their relatives, connections, and their native land, must be taken into the account … Enough of this horrid scene.[2]

The Quakers at Work

A Protestant for his entire life, Newton became a clergyman after turning from the slave trade. One of his primary arguments for abolition was that God was strictly against the slave trade. Other abolitionists used similar arguments, but no one was more influential in turning people of faith against the slave trade than the Society of Friends, better known as the Quakers. The Quakers, who believed in the spiritual equality of all humans including enslaved people, were particularly numerous and vocal in Great Britain and colonial America. At first, a number of Quakers enslaved Africans and merely advocated treating them humanely. By the late 1760s, however, the Quakers were advocating the more radical idea of freeing all those presently in servitude. In a meeting held in Philadelphia, Pennsylvania, in the late 18th century, American Quaker leaders urged the church to excommunicate (expel) members who did not free the enslaved people working for them.

The Quakers were noteworthy for their groundbreaking work toward eliminating the slave trade through political persuasion and new laws. Abolitionist organizations founded by Quakers gained supporters in Great Britain, France, and the United States in the 1780s. These groups produced and distributed pamphlets condemning the slave trade, organized boycotts against merchants who supported the trade, and urged politicians to introduce legislation banning the trade. Particularly influential was Thomas Clarkson. Though not a Quaker himself, he allied himself with leading Quakers and

FROM THE SOURCE: A LETTER FROM JOHN NEWTON

As a former British slave trader, John Newton had a view of the institution of slavery from the inside. He worked on slave ships, nearly losing his life in a storm at sea in 1748. He later credited God for saving his life and giving him faith in a famous hymn he wrote called "Amazing Grace."

A few years after the storm at sea, Newton gave up the profitable trade and became a minister. In 1788, he began writing and speaking out about his transition to the abolitionists' side in order to bolster the efforts of the British abolition movement to ban the slave trade. In a letter to a close friend in 1792, Newton explained how he looked at slavery differently after he realized the horrors of slavery:

I regarded it [slavery] not in a political, but in a moral view. I consider myself bound in conscience to bear my testimony at least, and to wash my hands from the Abolitionist John Newton served as a minister at St. Peter and Paul Church in Olney, England, from 1764 to 1780.

guilt which, if persisted in now that things have been so thoroughly investigated and brought to light, will, I think, constitute a national sin of a scarlet and crimson dye.[1]

1. Quoted in Gomer Williams, *History of the Liverpool Privateers and Letters of Marque, with an Account of the Liverpool Slave Trade* (London, UK: William Heinemann, 1897), p. 521.

forcefully lobbied members of the British Parliament to pass laws restricting and destroying the slave trade.

Among the legislators Clarkson worked with and influenced was William Wilberforce, a young evangelical Christian who became a member of Parliament in 1780. A vigorous opponent of the slave trade, Wilberforce became Great Britain's most famous and most vocal abolitionist. His repeated efforts to ban the trade first resulted in the 1788 Slave Trade Act (also called the Dolben Act), which set standards for conditions aboard British slave ships. In 1792, Wilberforce and his supporters managed to pass an outright ban of the trade in one of Parliament's two houses, the House of Commons. However, the other house, the more conservative House of Lords, called for a compromise of gradual abolition instead. It was now clear to all involved that the abolitionist movement was generating a forward motion that would be impossible to stop.

Uprisings

While British politicians argued over the benefits and downsides of the slave trade, the Americas saw increasing resistance and rebellions by the captive population. For decades, runaways in various parts of the Caribbean and Central and South America had banded together with other Africans trying to escape their enslavement. They had formed secret societies, often named maroon communities, that thrived in inaccessible wilderness areas. Members of these societies sometimes helped others escape from plantations.

As maroon communities grew larger in the late 1700s, large-scale uprisings became more common in colonial holdings. In 1763, enslaved people launched an insurrection and nearly took over the Dutch colony of Guyana in South America. The largest and most influential rebellion by enslaved people in history took place in the French colony of Saint-Domingue. Local maroon communities began regularly raiding white-owned plantations there in the 1780s. Then, in August 1791, an immense maroon-led uprising exploded in the northern sector of the colony. Its leader, Boukman Dutty, declared:

> The god who created the sun which gives us light, who rouses the waves and rules the storm … he watches us. He sees all that the white man does. The god of the white man inspires him with crime, but our god calls upon us to do good works. Our god … will direct our arms and aid us … listen to the voice of liberty, which speaks in the hearts of us all.[3]

Formerly enslaved people often helped each other. This 19th-century etching depicts men who have escaped slavery hiding in a swamp in Louisiana.

The rebellion soon spread throughout the colony. Other Black leaders rose from among the enslaved population, the most famous being Toussaint Louverture and Jean-Jacques Dessalines. These men led the rebels in a number of shocking military victories over the French colonial powers. In 1804, Saint-Domingue became the independent nation of Haiti, with a government run by formerly enslaved people. This event had a huge impact on the slave trade because many wealthy European merchants now feared that similar rebellions would become commonplace. That would make investing large sums of money in the trade much too risky a venture. Increasingly, enslavers began to perceive that the potential financial losses of the slave trade might outweigh its possible financial gains.

Taking on the Trade

The success of the slave revolt in what is now Haiti in the first years of the 1800s gave new strength to the abolitionist movement, especially in Great Britain and the United States. The British Empire abolished the slave trade in all its territories by an act of

HISTORY HAPPENED HERE: THE GREAT DISMAL SWAMP

The Great Dismal Swamp is a large marshy region with areas of dense forest in southeastern Virginia and northeastern North Carolina. It was given its name by Colonel William Byrd II in 1728 while he was trying to find the border between the two states. Of the area, which he disliked, he said, "It is certain many slaves shelter themselves in this obscure part of the world."[1]

The region's inhospitable nature is what made it a welcoming home to large numbers of freedom seekers. They constructed huts on the high ground of the swamp and used the animals that lived there as sources of food and clothing. Some even found work by taking jobs offered by nearby lumber businesses. Occasionally, slave catchers made journeys into the area, but they found it to be difficult to pass through. It is thought that some maroon communities survived in the swamp until the end of the American Civil War, when freedom was granted to all enslaved people in the nation.

1. Quoted in Richard Grant, "Deep in the Swamps, Archaeologists Are Finding How Fugitive Slaves Kept Their Freedom," *Smithsonian Magazine*, September 2016, www.smithsonianmag.com/history/deep-swamps-archaeologists-fugitive-slaves-kept-freedom-180960122/.

Parts of the Great Dismal Swamp are like islands rising above the marshy land. These made it possible for freedom seekers to successfully live in communities within the swamp.

Born into slavery, Toussaint Louverture was freed in 1776 and worked to free others in Haiti. He also helped orchestrate the freeing of people in neighboring Santo Domingo (today's Dominican Republic) in 1801.

Parliament in 1807. Also in 1807, legislators in the United States Congress, supported by President Thomas Jefferson, passed a law forbidding further importation of enslaved Africans after January 1, 1808.

Other nations followed suit. In 1811, Spain abolished slavery, including in all its colonies except Cuba. Three years later, the Netherlands banned slave trading. Though France did the same in 1817, it was not effective until 1826. Great Britain persuaded Portugal to limit their slave ships to trading routes south of the equator beginning in 1819.

It was not long, however, before Great Britain resorted to more aggressive measures to stop the few remaining countries that dealt in the slave trade. The British West Africa Squadron was a group of warships that began patrolling the area around Africa's West Coast. These vessels hunted down and captured slave ships from other nations. At first reluctantly, France and the United States joined this effort. Slave traders now became the equivalent of international pirates. Tens of thousands of Africans were reportedly liberated by these fleets of antislavery ships.

One of these freed men was a Nigerian named Ajayi, who took the name Samuel Crowther after gaining his freedom. He had been captured at around age 15 in 1821. Taken to the coast on a slow journey of almost two years, he was sold to a Portuguese slave trader and placed on a ship as part of the transatlantic slave trade's final years. Ajayi was chained to several other African boys and men, who were forced to lie close together in a small room in the hold. Fortunately for Ajayi and his companions, a group of British vessels

PAST MEETS PRESENT: REENACTMENT OF THE 1811 GERMAN COAST SLAVE UPRISING

The largest slave revolt in U.S. history began on a plantation in an area called the German Coast of Louisiana. A man named Charles Deslondes led a group of enslaved people into the house of plantation owner Manuel Andry. They injured Andry and killed his son. Next, possibly inspired by the uniforms of the Haitian revolt, they put on Andry's militia uniforms. Armed with some of the plantation owner's weapons as well as farm tools, they marched toward New Orleans, gathering more than 500 enslaved people, burning down plantations and chanting, "Freedom or death!" Their hope was to establish a free state for Black people along the banks of the Mississippi River. A militia stopped the revolters, though, killing 45 of them. About 50 more were hung or shot later, and the heads of some were placed on poles along the road to New Orleans.

In 2019, hundreds of people in Louisiana reenacted the event by marching along much of the same route as the rebels had during their uprising. Artist Dread Scott organized the event, saying, "In addition to our country grappling with the long-reaching, present-day effects of slavery and oppression, it is important to acknowledge the power that resides in reimagining your own destiny. We can learn a great deal from the many stories of that era."[1]

1. Quoted in Edmund D. Fountain, "Reenacting the Largest Slave Revolt in US History," CNN.com, November 10, 2019, www.cnn.com/2019/11/10/us/gallery/slave-rebellion-reenactment/index.html.

suddenly appeared and captured the slave ship and its owners. "In a few days we were quite at home in the man-of-war [British ship]," Ajayi later wrote. "[We] were soon furnished with clothes. Our

THEY MADE HISTORY: WILLIAM WILBERFORCE

William Wilberforce was among the world's leading advocates of the abolition of the transatlantic slave trade in the late 1700s and early 1800s. Born into a wealthy British family in Yorkshire, England, on August 24, 1759, he was strongly influenced by abolitionist crusaders in his teenage years—especially John Newton. Wilberforce decided to use his wealth and influence to fight against the trade. To achieve this goal, he managed to become a member of Parliament when he was 21. He lobbied his fellow legislators constantly to speak out against the slave trade and led the Committee for the Abolition of the Slave Trade, introducing abolition bills frequently until one finally passed the House of Commons in 1792. Although the House of Lords vetoed the bill, Wilberforce refused to give up. The bill that ended the slave trade finally passed both houses of Parliament in 1807. Having achieved this great milestone, he then devoted himself untiringly to the abolition of slavery as a whole. William Wilberforce died on July 29, 1833, one month before the Slavery Abolition Act was passed in Great Britain.

Portuguese owner and his son were brought over into the same vessel, bound in fetters; and, thinking that I should no more get into his hand, I had the boldness to strike him on the head."[4] The British not only treated the captured slave trader harshly—by chaining and imprisoning him—but also took his vessel completely out of commission. Ajayi remembered seeing the British sailors strip off the ship's rigging and abandon it at sea, its certain fate to sink into nothingness beneath the waves.

Ceasing Slavery Itself

With the pillars of the transatlantic slave trade crumbling, the abolitionists refocused on the institution of slavery itself. Even though people were no longer being transported legally to many colonies and countries, millions were trapped in a life of suffering and servitude. Also, according to laws in many places, their children would be too.

With the efforts of the abolition movement, the law began to change with the changing perspectives of people. England, once the major player in the triangular trade, was one of the first to abolish slavery. The British Parliament banned slavery in most of its empire in 1833, and the ban went into effect on August 1, 1834. Instead of an immediate emancipation, though, enslaved people over the age of six had to serve an apprenticeship of four to six years (though this was abolished in 1838).

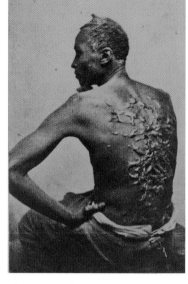

This man, showing his scars from whippings, escaped a life of slavery to fight for the Union army during the American Civil War.

Soon, the institution fell in other nations and colonies. In 1846, Denmark abolished slavery in the Danish West Indies. In 1848, France abolished it. Ten years later, Portugal abolished slavery in its colonies, thereafter forcing enslaved people into a 20-year apprenticeship. In 1861, the Netherlands abolished slavery in its Caribbean colonies.

Slavery was the driving force behind the American Civil War in the United States, which began in 1861. After the victory of the Union in 1865, slavery was abolished that same year through the Thirteenth Amendment to the U.S. Constitution. Cuba finally abolished slavery in 1886. Brazil (which had become independent from Portugal in 1822) was the last country in the Americas to abolish slavery, which happened in 1888.

Aftereffects

Though the transatlantic slave trade was eliminated by the end of the 19th century and legalized slavery itself came to an end, centuries of abuse and human rights violations would have an impact for decades to come. In many parts of the world, slavery's consequences are still being played out. In Africa, the transatlantic slave trade caused damages that may never be repaired. Because warring tribes were the source of countless numbers of Africans being sold into slavery, the cultural norms of the entire continent were corrupted. A cycle of war and unsustainable economic practices—particularly after the slave trade was abolished—made many African countries weak and vulnerable to colonialism and civil war. The slave trade likely cost African nations their chance at developing strong agricultural and industrial economies earlier. According to Ghanaian historian Zagba Oyortey, "During slavery many of the able-bodied people, between 18 and 40, were taken out so society's ability to reproduce itself economically, socially and culturally was impaired."[5] The wake of destruction on the continent of Africa cannot be overestimated.

The opposite was true in Europe and the Americas. There, population growth had significantly increased over the centuries. The main cause was the sharp increase in agricultural production—supported by millions of enslaved people—including basic food crops in the Americas. Partly because of these population increases in Europe and the Americas, many nations in these regions expanded their holdings, both abroad and at home. This was accomplished either through colonization (as in the case of England establishing colonies across the globe) or conquest of nearby lands (as in the case of the United States absorbing Native American lands in its expansion to the West Coast). The economic, political, and military successes of these nations were, therefore, indirectly a result of the inexpensive labor and massive food production of millions of enslaved people. This food kept colonists content, populations explosive, and armies fed. Without being supported by millions of African laborers, America may never have evolved past its 13 original states.

Turbulent Times

In the 21st century, scholars are still debating the large-scale economic, demographic, and political effects of the transatlantic slave trade. However, most people can see the obvious and destructive effects in the troubling racial tensions in the United States and across the world. Some activists and academics have argued that the descendants of enslaved Africans are still feeling the effects of the slave trade. Racism, despite more than a century having passed since the worldwide abolition of slavery, is still rampant, especially in America and Europe. This is because the broad acceptance of people of African descent is still a relatively recent development; until the late 1900s, many white people still widely considered Black people to be inferior. The result is racial discrimination, unfair laws, and widespread poverty among Black citizens in many countries.

In the United States, the civil rights movement—which rose to prominence during the 1950s—helped reduce some of these social inequalities. A Supreme Court victory in the 1954 case *Brown v. Board of Education of Topeka* established that segregation in schools was unconstitutional. In the 1960s, the movement successfully promoted passage of key laws to combat discrimination in public places and at the voting booth too. Despite the numerous achievements of the civil rights movement, however, there are still major race-related issues that plague America.

The social movement called Black Lives Matter formed in the United States in 2013, following the shooting of Black teenager Trayvon Martin and the acquittal of the man who killed him. Black Lives Matter became a leading force in organizing community protests against racial inequality in the American criminal justice system. In 2020, a video surfaced that showed a Minneapolis police officer killing an unarmed Black man named George Floyd by kneeling on his neck. In response, Black Lives Matter protests erupted across the country and spread into other nations that shared outrage against institutional racism. Black people and their allies demanded change in the laws and organizations that allowed such brutality against people of color.

Some believe this racism is the ghost of slavery still haunting modern culture and that until slavery's legacies are truly recognized and dealt with, senseless deaths of innocent Black Americans will continue to happen.

Noted historian and scholar Henry Louis Gates Jr. wrote:

Until we as a society fully reckon with the history of slavery in all its dimensions ... and overcome our historical denial of the

At different times in U.S. history, there have been calls for change to address systemic injustice toward Black Americans.

central shaping role that slavery has played in the creating of all of America's social, political, cultural, and economic institutions, we cannot truly begin to confront the so-called race problem in this country.[6]

Undoubtedly, every country that took part in the slave trade still feels its effects in some way. Such a long-lasting and deep-rooted institution as slavery could not be neatly "solved" with laws of abolition. Centuries later, we are still grappling with slavery's remnants of racism and violence. The wounds have not yet healed.

How You See History

1. Why do you think slave rebellions are not a major part of American history education?

2. Do you think Haiti's slave revolt had an impact on slavery in other places? Why?

3. How are the effects of slavery still felt in the United States and around the world today?

TIMELINE

1444

The Portuguese transport 235 enslaved people from West Africa to Lagos, Portugal.

1492

Sailing for Spain, Italian explorer Christopher Columbus lands in what are now the Bahamas and islands in the Caribbean, initiating a European rush to exploit the Americas.

1607

British settlers land in Jamestown, in what becomes the colony of Virginia.

1619

Twenty enslaved people arrive in Virginia, the first Africans shipped to the British North American colonies.

1627

British settlers, including enslaved Africans, arrive on the island of Barbados, which is a British colony.

1781

The captain of the British slave ship *Zong* throws more than 130 captive Africans overboard, igniting loud protests by abolitionists.

1804

After a successful slave revolt, Saint-Domingue becomes the independent nation of Haiti, with a government run by formerly enslaved people.

1807

Great Britain bans the slave trade.

1808
The United States abolishes the slave trade. Great Britain creates an antislavery squadron of warships to patrol in the Atlantic.

1833
The British Empire abolishes slavery in most of its colonies around the world.

1861
The American Civil War begins; slavery is a main cause of the conflict.

1865
The Union wins the American Civil War. The Thirteenth Amendment to the U.S. Constitution bans slavery in the United States.

1888
Brazil becomes the last country in the Americas to abolish slavery.

1954
The civil rights movement organizes to fight for Black citizens' civil rights in the United States, beginning with a ruling by the U.S. Supreme Court asserting that segregated schools are unconstitutional.

1964
The civil rights movement gains a victory with the passage of the Civil Rights Act, which outlaws discrimination against Black Americans in public places.

1965
The Voting Rights Act ends restrictions on voting meant to keep Black Americans from exercising their right to vote.

2013
The social movement called Black Lives Matter emerges among protests condemning violence against Black Americans, seeking reforms to combat institutional racism.

NOTES

Introduction: A Terrible Part of History

1. Hakim Adi, Alik Shahadah, and Kimani Nehusi, "Transatlantic Slave Trade," African Holocaust, December 2005, www.africanholocaust. net/articles/TRANSATLANTIC%20SLAVE%20TRADE.htm.

2. Anne C. Bailey, *African Voices of the Atlantic Slave Trade: Beyond the Silence and the Shame* (Boston, MA: Beacon Press, 2005), p. 227.

3. Maulana Karenga, "The Ethics of Reparations: Engaging the Holocaust of Enslavement," N'COBRA, accessed June 9, 2020, www. ncobraonline.org/wp-content/uploads/2016/02/Karenga-THE-ETHICS-OF-REPARATIONS.pdf.

4. Bailey, pp. 230, 231.

Chapter One: The Spread of Slavery

1. Quoted in "Transatlantic Slave Trade 'One of the Greatest Atrocities in History,' Says Secretary-General at International Day Commemoration," UN.org, March 25, 2008, www.un.org/press/en/2008/sgsm11479.doc. htm.

2. Stuart B. Schwartz, *Slaves, Peasants, and Rebels: Reconsidering Brazilian Slavery* (Urbana, IL: University of Illinois Press, 1996), p. 40.

3. Gomes Eanes de Zurara, *The Chronicle of the Discovery and Conquest of Guinea*, trans. Charles Raymond Beazley and Edgar Prestage (New York, NY: Cambridge University Press, 2010), p. 85.

4. Quoted in Ellie Cawthorne, "History Explorer: The British Slave Trade," HistoryExtra, March 17, 2018, www.historyextra.com/period/ georgian/history-explorer-the-british-slave-trade/.

Chapter Two: Colonial Labor

1. Howard Zinn, *A People's History of the United States: 1492–Present* (New York, NY: HarperCollins, 2005), p. 25.

2. Quoted in Zinn, p. 25.

3. Ulrich Bonnell Phillips, *American Negro Slavery: A Survey of the Supply, Employment and Control of Negro Labor as Determined by the Plantation Regime* (New York, NY: D. Appleton and Company, 1918), pp. 39–40.

4. Quoted in Hugh Thomas, *The Slave Trade: The Story of the Atlantic Slave Trade, 1440–1870* (New York, NY: Simon & Schuster, 1997), p. 431.

5. "Colonial Virginia Laws on Slavery and Servitude," HERB: Resources for Teachers, herb.ashp.cuny.edu/items/show/863 (accessed May 27, 2020).

Chapter Three: Captive in Africa

1. John Newton, "Thoughts Upon the African Slave Trade," Wikisource, en.wikisource.org/wiki/Thoughts_upon_the_African_Slave_Trade (accessed June 9, 2020).

2. Quoted in K. G. Davies, *The North Atlantic World in the Seventeenth Century* (Minneapolis, MN: University of Minnesota Press, 1974), p. 253.

3. Olaudah Equiano, *The Interesting Narrative of the Life of Olaudah Equiano, or Gustavus Vassa, the African*, vol. 1 (1789; Documenting the American South, 2001), pp. 48–49, docsouth.unc.edu/neh/equiano1/equiano1.html.

4. Mungo Park, *Life and Travels of Mungo Park in Central Africa* (Project Gutenberg, 2005), chap. 24, www.gutenberg.org/cache/epub/8564/pg8564.html.

5. Park, chap. 26.

Chapter Four: The Middle Passage

1. Quoted in Anthony Benezet, *Some Historical Account of Guinea* (Frankfurt, Germany: Outlook, 2019), p. 61.

2. Olaudah Equiano, *The Interesting Narrative of the Life of Olaudah Equiano, or Gustavus Vassa, the African*, vol. 1 (1789; Documenting the American South, 2001), pp. 73–74, docsouth.unc.edu/neh/equiano1/equiano1.html.

3. Quoted in Howard Zinn, *A People's History of the United States: 1492–Present* (New York, NY: HarperCollins, 2005), p. 29.

4. Equiano, pp. 78–79.

5. Equiano, pp. 81–82.

6. Quoted in Edward L. Ayers, et al., *American Passages: A History of the United States Vol. 1: To 1877* (Boston, MA: Wadsworth, 2010), pp. 74–75.

Chapter Five: Into a Life of Slavery

1. Olaudah Equiano, *The Interesting Narrative of the Life of Olaudah Equiano, or Gustavus Vassa, the African*, vol. 1 (1789; Documenting the American South, 2001), p. 85, docsouth.unc.edu/neh/equiano1/equiano1.html.

2. Equiano, pp. 86–87.

3. Quoted in R. P. Forster, ed., *A Collection of the Most Celebrated Voyages and Travels, From the Discovery of America to the Present Time*, vol. 2 (Newcastle upon Tyne, UK: Mackenzie and Dent, 1818), p. 44.

4. Equiano, pp. 93–94.

5. Equiano, pp. 91–92.

6. Quoted in Harriet Beecher Stowe, *Dred: A Tale of the Great Dismal Swamp*, ed. Robert S. Levine (Chapel Hill, NC: University of North Carolina Press, 2006), p. 572.

Chapter Six: The Abolition Movement

1. John Newton, "Thoughts Upon the African Slave Trade," Wikisource, en.wikisource.org/wiki/Thoughts_upon_the_African_Slave_Trade (accessed June 9, 2020).

2. John Newton, "Motives to Humiliation and Praise: A Sermon" (London, UK: J. Johnson, 1798), p. 23.

3. Quoted in Jared Hickman, *Black Prometheus: Race and Radicalism in the Age of Atlantic Slavery* (New York, NY: Oxford University Press, 2017), PDF e-book, p. 66.

4. Quoted in William H. Worger, et al., *Africa and the West: From the Slave Trade to Conquest, 1441–1905* (Oxford, UK: Oxford University Press, 2010), p. 109.

5. Quoted in Will Ross, "Slavery's Long Effects on Africa," BBC News, March 29, 2007, news.bbc.co.uk/2/hi/africa/6504141.stm.

6. Quoted in Rachael Hanel, *The Slave Trade* (Mankato, MN: Creative Education, 2008), PDF e-book, p. 44.

FOR MORE INFORMATION

Books: Nonfiction

Caravantes, Peggy. *Escaping Slavery*. North Mankato, MN: The Child's World, 2019.

Harris, Duchess, and Marcia Amidon Lusted. *The Transatlantic Slave Trade*. Minneapolis, MN: Abdo Publishing, 2020.

Proenza-Coles, Christina. *American Founders: How People of African Descent Established Freedom in the New World*. Montgomery, AL: NewSouth Books, 2019.

Shally-Jensen, Michael. *Slavery*. Ipswich, MA: Salem Press, 2019.

Books: Fiction

Attah, Ayesha Harruna. *The Hundred Wells of Salaga*. New York, NY: Other Press, 2019.

Gyasi, Yaa. *Homegoing*. New York, NY: Knopf, 2016.

Saul, Quincy, ed. *Maroon Comix: Origins and Destinies*. Oakland, CA: PM Press, 2018.

Stowe, Harriet Beecher. *Uncle Tom's Cabin*. London, UK: Macmillan Collector's Library, 2020.

Websites

A History of Slavery in the United States
www.nationalgeographic.org/interactive/slavery-united-states/
An interactive timeline allows people to understand the chronology of certain important events in this dark subject of history.

Pre–Civil War African-American Slavery
www.loc.gov/teachers/classroommaterials/presentationsandactivities/presentations/timeline/expref/slavery/
Find information about this time period as well as primary source documents on this Library of Congress website.

Slavery in America
www.history.com/topics/black-history/slavery
Read a short history of slavery in the Western Hemisphere, starting in 1619, compiled by the editors of History.com.

Slave Voyages
www.slavevoyages.org
Discover this valuable collection of information about the transatlantic slave trade and the suffering endured by captured Africans on the high seas.

INDEX

PHOTO CREDITS

Cover adoc-photos/Contributor/Corbis Historical/Getty Images; pp. 4, 16, 56 Interim Archives/Contributor/Archive Photos/Getty Images; p. 8 Archive Photos/Stringer/Archive Photos/Getty Images; p. 9 Raymond Boyd/Contributor/Michael Ochs Archives/Getty Images; pp. 10, 34 Print Collector/Contributor/Hulton Archive/Getty Images; p. 18 Everett Collection/Shutterstock.com; p. 19 The MET/ Gift of J. Pierpont Morgan, 1900; p. 22 Victor Metelskiy/iStock/Getty Images Plus/Getty Images; p. 24 Anadolu Agency/Contributor/Anadolu Agency/Getty Images; pp. 27, 71 Jeff Greenberg/Contributor/Universal Images Group/Getty Images; p. 31 Kean Collection/Staff/Archive Photos/Getty Images; p. 32 Stock Montage/Contributor/Archive Photos/Getty Images; p. 38 Bardocz Peter/Shutterstock.com; p. 42 Werner Forman/Contributor/Universal Images Group/Getty Images; p. 44 UniversalImagesGroup/Contributor/Universal Images Group/ Getty Images; p. 45 Photo Josse/Leemage/Contributor/Corbis Historical/Getty Images; p. 47 Courtesy of the British Library; pp. 49, 50, 88 Courtesy of the Library of Congress; pp. 54, 83 Smith Collection/ Gado/Contributor/Archive Photos/Getty Images; pp. 57, 66 MPI/ Stringer/Archive Photos/Getty Images; p. 59 Historical/Contributor/ Corbis Historical/Getty Images; p. 61 Hulton Archive/Stringer/Hulton Archive/Getty Images; p. 62 DEA/A. Dagli Orti/Contributor/De Agostini/Getty Images; p. 68 ullstein bild Dtl./Contributor/ullstein bild/Getty Images; p. 69 Rischgitz/Stringer/Hulton Archive/Getty Images; p. 74 Photo 12/Contributor/Universal Images Group/Getty Images; p. 75 Universal History Archive/Contributor/Universal Images Group/Getty Images; p. 76 Time Life Pictures/Contributor/The LIFE Picture Collection/Getty Images; pp. 81, 85 Hulton Archive Stringer/Archive Photos/Getty Images; p. 84 Sean Russell/Getty Images; p. 91 (left) Bettmann/Contributor/Bettmann/Getty Images; p. 91 (right) Mario Tama/Staff/Getty Images News/Getty Images.

ABOUT THE AUTHOR

Therese Harasymiw has written and edited more than 300 nonfiction books for children and teens, including works on slave rebellions, the American Civil War, and biographies of renowned African Americans. Harasymiw received an English degree from Providence College and a master of education degree in English education from the State University of New York at Buffalo. A former high school literature teacher, she works as a senior editor in educational publishing. Harasymiw, her husband, and their two children reside in Rochester, New York.